Breaking Through Boundaries

Lisa Beth Adams

DEDICATION

This book is dedicated to setting captives free from the limiting power of boundaries we were never meant to have and to help people grow into a higher place in living and loving well.

CONTENTS

ACKNOWLEDGMENTS

I want to say thank you to Joel Sweeney for being my brother by choice. For prophesying that I would write this book and for helping me to grow along the way until I could. You have been one of my greatest sources of encouragement. I wouldn't be who I am today if it weren't for you and your extraordinary relationship with our Father.

I wish to thank my friend Michael Van Vlyman for not only his encouragement, but for helping me learn how to create my book covers and self publish my creations.

Thanks goes to Judy Lynn Claussen for helping me by editing. You are an absolute blessing to me! Thank you for partnering with me for the Lords work.

Thank you to all my friends and family who have believed in me. I cherish you.

Introduction

I saw a woman who stood in the face of God and said; "How big are You?" God replied; "I AM." And He showed her some of His power. It came as a gentle rain, the wind blew a little and the earth received change and life.

The woman saw the rain and wind and said; "This is amazing!" She delighted in it for a season but soon it wasn't enough. I saw the woman stand in the face of God and say; "That was nice, but is that all you've got?" And God replied; "I AM." And in His delight in her, He sent a storm. The storm had peals of thunder and lightning. The wind was stronger and caused some damage. Tree branches broke off and minor damages happened to her house. The woman saw what the Lord had done and said; "Wow! That was powerful!" She felt confused for a bit and had to do some research to learn how to clean up the downed branches and fixed the damage on her house.

As time passed, she watched the new growth come on the trees and the grass turn green with refreshment. Flowers bloomed everywhere and the sun had again come out. When her house was back in order, she looked up at God and said; "That was pretty impressive. You set me back a bit, but things look better now than before. But really Lord, is that all you've got?"

So the Lord again looked at His daughter and said, "I AM". This time He sent a strong tornado and straight line winds that tore down entire trees. He tore her house in half and destroyed half of all she owned. This time, the woman cried and lamented for a time. She didn't have the tools to fix her place and her home on her own. She would seek God for instructions, so God sent her friends to help her restore her home. They would tell her they thought the foundation was weak in areas, so she patched the foundation with the word of God thinking that would strengthen the current foundation and it would be alright. She was trying to understand why there was so much destruction? It seemed overwhelming, and this time it was much more difficult to restore and rebuild. But once the work was done, the house looked better than before. Some trees survived and grew new branches. Some trees had been completely uprooted.

As time passed, she forgot the pain of the strong storm and as she looked at God, she felt like something was missing. She was still thinking there had to be something more. So once again, the woman stood in the face of God and said; "IS THAT ALL YOU'VE GOT?"

And God, knowing her heart was not speaking from arrogance or pride, but of a sincere desire to know just how powerful her Father in heaven was, once again said; "I AM". This time, He sent people to warn her. You better either buckle down hard or flee. There is a huge price to pay if you stay here and endure what God is about to do. She looked at the people and said; "I choose to stay. I will pay the price." The people ministered to her, taught her how to stand in the face of what was to come and prepared her the best they knew how.
Then the storm came. It was a mighty hurricane. The forces of the winds and rain came so hard that nothing she had was left standing. Her house was completely destroyed and the foundation crushed. Every tree was uprooted. Not even she was left standing.

***

No one ever told me how incredible having a relationship with Christ could be. Not like this. Not like what you are about to read in this book. But looking at it now, I'm not sure anyone *could* explain in words what it is like. How do you explain a feeling; a state of being; a life experience? How do you explain love? Not philia love, but agape love. God is so vast, so deep, so wide, so high that learning of His ways and love is endless.

Prior to now, I knew only religion. I was told, Jesus was the savior of the world and that by accepting Him it meant I would get to go to heaven when I died. I heard that there was no pain or sorrow there--no more tears would flood my cheeks from the many pains of this life. These were all things to look forward to in the future. Meaning, meeting Christ had to wait until that day--the day I died.

This seemed so far off. So distant, and yet this hope for heaven became the fuel that kept me trying to 'stay saved'.

I came to Christ when I was 13 years old. I remember how light and happy I felt after accepting Him. In those younger years, clear up into my late 30's, I believed that my goal in life was to do my best to be good and not sin so I could stay in God's good graces. I feared God. But not the right kind of fear. While the churches I had attended all spoke about how loving God was, the message that always stood out more strongly was, "sinners go to hell." God hates sin and so in my mind, every time I messed up or missed the mark, God was mad at me, and I just couldn't be good enough to keep Him happy. I felt like a failure.

I saw how harsh God appeared in the old testament and just couldn't wrap my mind around how God could change so much from the old testament to the new. He was supposed to be the same yesterday, today and forever right? I was told, Jesus was the full expression of God in bodily form. It just didn't make sense. Jesus was so amazing, so compassionate, and a healer. I felt like there was good-cop bad-cop thing going on. Jesus was the good cop always telling mean ole God that He paid the price for my sins so God should relent from crushing me like a bug and sending me to hell. God seemed angry, harsh and distant to me. I didn't see Him as a God of love, but a God of raging fire and anger. It seemed that the only loving act He did was sending Jesus to save me from *Him* sending me to hell!

I'm just being real here folks. Prior to 2009, no one who saw me would ever know the turmoil I had in my spirit trying to understand God and Jesus. The Holy Spirit was a whole other topic that had to be sorted through. I wore the mask of religion well. I expressed outwardly to others what I "hoped" was true about the bible and Jesus. I looked happy and that life was peas and carrots. But when I was alone with myself, I battled depression and confusion. My emotions were a roller coaster of ups and downs. You know what I'm talking about. When you're up, you are really up and when you're down, you are really down.

I had no idea that In April of 2009 while sitting alone in the Church of Christ sanctuary, I would ask God a question that would spark the beginning of what has now been the most incredible decade of my life! This is a journey from fearing God, to trusting Him; from an average life of the hypocrite Christian (professing my Christianity but battling living a sinful life) to a life of seeing miracles, healings and prophetic words flowing. It included being physically touched by angels and demons, and casting out devils and seeing incredible deliverance; feeling God's power on me when I pray, being able to feel other people's emotions both when I am in front of them or far away, hearing people's hearts speak to me, knowing things about strangers I have never met, and more. But friends, I am here to tell you--all of that is RUBBISH compared to what I found in my new relationship with my Heavenly Father, with Jesus my brother and Holy Spirit my teacher! But combined, it is a life on earth full of awe and wonder as God and I co-labor in revealing Him to the world.

I kept a journal of many of the incredible testimonies and encounters I've experienced with God as I grew, walking out my new found faith in Him for the miraculous. I put them together and created a book titled, "My Supernatural Life". It's not a book to boast. It was written so others could read my experiences with God after I had changed what I believed in my heart. It took overcoming all the boundaries you will read in this book (and many others) to produce what you will read in that one. Maybe you are dealing with some of the same boundaries. And maybe you will move on to experience all you will read in "My Supernatural Life". It's all about revealing Jesus. It's all about what you believe in your heart.

I am the woman who stood in the face of God and asked how big He was. He had to completely destroy the very foundations of who I thought I was and what I believed as truth. He had to knock me off my feet. I had to rebuild from scratch.

I learned over the course of the last 10 years, it was these many boundaries that held me back from becoming what I saw in some Christians whom I esteemed. Because of my wrong mindsets and wrong heart condition, I chased after wrong things before God guided me into a better way.

I can share all my mistakes with you here without shame or guilt or concern about my reputation, because as you will see when you traverse this book, God healed my heart of all shame or guilt. He healed me of having a need to have a reputation of my own. I have learned to live a surrendered life. This gives me the freedom to lay my life out for all to see in hopes that others will grow from my life journey. When you live surrendered, you will find absolute acceptance in Him. He will affirm you. If needed, He will correct you and guide you deeper into truth. He continues to teach me what boundaries lay in the way and shows me how to overcome them. He will do this for you as well. This is the refiners fire we all hear so much about. And yes, at times that fire can be painful! But each time He puts us in there and cranks the heat up hotter and hotter, the dross is burned off and we come out bearing His reflection! It's so worth it!

God is so amazing in that He started using me in ministry while He was yet refining me, long before I got my thoughts about Him corrected. It was truly a journey of awe and wonder as He drew me in so gently, baby step by baby step with a few giant leaps along the way, into the depths of His love; not only for me but for all He has made and all that He is. And it just keeps unfolding...

If you picked up this book, it is probably because you are seeking the bigger things. God will redefine what a bigger thing is if you hang around Him long enough. Every time I thought I knew what was a big thing--having a gift or ability or ministry etc--He would set me free from yet another boundary, and my paradox would change. The gifts of God are awesome! But by the grace of God, He taught me the more. There is more friends! The gifts and workings of God are a BYPRODUCT of being with Him. The more we are with Him--in His presence, in relationship with Him, being obedient to what He has asked us to do, and then walk it out by faith--they just start to happen.

Join me as I share my story with you.

I am confident that you will see yourself in areas of my walk and you too will gain freedom with what Christ has taught to me. The first two chapters (Boundaries) carry parts of the old foundation that needed to be torn down. By chapter 3, I will explain the boundaries more and share how to overcome them.

In accepting Jesus Christ, God's only Son, as your Savior, you have been given all the power and authority in Jesus' name to change the world. His Holy Spirit will live in you, giving you power to heal the sick, raise the dead and set the captives free! More importantly, He gives you the power to be free in a tangible relationship with Himself. Journey with me as we begin Breaking Through Boundaries that hem us in.

Boundary 1: The Power Of God Not For Today

I tell you the truth, anyone who believes in me will do the same works I have done, and even greater works, because I am going to be with the Father. John 14:12 NLT

I started attending a Church of Christ with the sole purpose being to get my husband to come with me to church and for him to get saved. He had relatives that attended there so I hoped he would come if only to see them.

I was 27 at the time and still working on getting myself right with God. This church taught the bible and loved God. The people there are very loving and full of hospitality. I adored our first pastor as he preached with a heart that loved God and His word. The church services on Sundays were traditional and predictable. Meaning, you knew how things were going to go, in order, every Sunday. At this stage in my walk with God, this was comforting and made me feel stability in my life. I was starving for God so I attended every single bible teaching that was available. I was there early and stayed late. I was there Sunday mornings, attended Sunday school, Sunday nights, Wednesday nights and read my bible at home. I was soaking up the Word like a sponge. After eleven years of marriage, John accepted the Lord! We were attending as a family and I was elated!

While I loved so many things about this church and my church family, something was still missing. I still felt like there was more. I felt an emptiness. I felt confined. The draw to know more about the supernatural, angels, demons and the power of God was coming back to life in me, and I wanted to understand it. What was a word of knowledge? What was prophecy? Why did God list those gifts in 1 Corinthians 12? How did you get them? Could women get them? The bible seemed like a man's world. If those things did happen, surely it wasn't for me. And yet, there were scriptures that would say, "I will pour out my Spirit on all people. Your sons and **daughters** will prophesy, your old men will dream dreams, your young men will see visions." Joel 2:28 (emphasis added) What did that mean? Was that for the end times? The church I was attending didn't believe there were prophets today, and I had never heard anyone speak a prophetic word. So where did that verse fit in?

In each church I attended, the theology was the same. My theology would be the first boundary God would have to clear from me. The teaching I received was that the power and gifts stopped with the Apostles in the early church. We could believe for a move of God or His mercy, but no one ever talked about walking in any of the gifts of the Spirit listed in 1 Corinthians 12. No one denied them per-say, but no one walked in them either. Here is the list of gifts listed:

8 To one there is given through the Spirit a message of wisdom, to another a message of knowledge by means of the same Spirit, 9 to another faith by the same Spirit, to another gifts of healing by that one Spirit, 10 to another miraculous powers, to another prophecy, to another distinguishing between spirits, to another speaking in different kinds of tongues, and to still another the interpretation of tongues. 11 All these are the work of one and the same Spirit, and he distributes them to each one, just as he determines.

1 Corinthians 12: 8-11 (NIV)

This all caused me to develop a question for God. I had been in the Church of Christ for 12 years now, and a year before asking the big question, I asked the leadership for a key to the church. I wanted to be able to come to the church and pray whenever I felt a need to. They entrusted me with a key and so began the season of coming to the sanctuary every morning for anywhere from an hour to three hours to pray and worship God. It was just Him and me.

From the very beginning of attending my beloved Church of Christ, I felt restrained. Like I had to suppress the me that was inside. Everyone stood so still during services. No one raised their hands in praise. It was very stoic. At that point, it was all old hymnals that were used. So, on these mornings of just God and me--I brought my own music. I danced for Him and I sang to Him from the deep places in my heart. At times I would stand at the pulpit and preach to the empty pews and prophesy over the people and the city.

I started having some experiences there alone with God. One time that really stands out, I had been singing and dancing for awhile, and sitting at the piano to pluck at it a little. I was feeling convicted of my speech and asked God if He would send that angel with the fiery hot coal to cleans my tongue and lips. All of a sudden my tongue started buzzing, and so did my lips. I was like, NO WAY!! It was time for me to leave and go to work, so I stood up to go and found myself drunk in my movements. My legs were wobbly and I needed to use the pews to support me as I tried to walk out. I WAS BY MYSELF! But God had met me in power and was loving on me! I had heard of this kind of stuff happening at large meetings with ministers anointed with the Holy Spirit praying over people, but *never* thought it possible to have it happen when alone with the Lord! This woke something in my heart. God is intimate, personal and needs no one to "bring Him in." He is omnipresent ...always present. All I was doing was worshiping Him and had faith in His word for myself.

The day of the question came. I was again alone in the sanctuary, kneeling on the floor before the altar. The call in my heart to know if God was still powerful was raging inside of me. In my searches for things of the supernatural, all through my youth, I could see the power of Satan everywhere. I could see people give themselves over to witchcraft, get demons assigned to them, then walk in amazing abilities and power. I had acquaintances who had done drugs in their past. They told me that they would actually see demons and get tortured by them. Even some of the homeless I would meet would tell me they experienced demons in this way. I had been in houses that had demonic activity in them and had no way to explain it away.

It seemed I could find the power of the dark side everywhere and that it was EASY for people to access it. This just did not make any sense to me. Where was the power of God? So, I asked Him. "Why do I see the power of the devil everywhere? Where Are You? Didn't You say that You were the same yesterday, today and forever? What does that mean? If You gave power to heal the sick and raise the dead to the baby church, where is that power now? Why don't I see it? Did it die with the apostles or is it still for today? It's not fair that the devils children can hear devils so clearly and walk in all kinds of power so readily. Where are You? How can we compete with what I am seeing from the dark side?"

OK--so it was more than one question. But this was THE moment that started the ball rolling that would change my life forever.

At that point in my walk, God seemed locked up in His book, the Bible. It was just information about Him, you had to wish and hope that He would move on your behalf.

After the questions, God started leading me to books like Maria Woodworth Etter, Smith Wigglesworth, Kathryn Kuhlman and the like. Notice, two of these were women!! Something else the Church taught me was that women had no real roles in the church other than Sunday school teacher and nursery attendant. The only scripture my mind could see at the time was that women were to be quiet in the church. This was a LOUD voice that kept me questioning God about these women I was reading about and others He would soon show me. I had never seen a woman allowed to speak at the pulpit and our church completely rejected women preachers or ministers. So the thought of it for myself felt VERY uncomfortable and yet it was in my daydreams almost daily. I *always* saw myself speaking on stages as a public speaker sharing about Jesus.

I could not read more than three pages in *any* of these books without sobbing. They touched something deep inside of me and gave me a strong hope that God was still doing miracles today! These were people lo-o-ong after the apostles that God was using mightily to work miracles and heal multitudes of people. This sparked an insatiable hunger in me to learn more. I read every book I could find. I dreamed about it night and day.

God began to teach me. I would soon meet a man who walked in faith for healing. He had a genuine gift, but his character was bad. This confused me for awhile. Why God would do great healing through a man who had shown himself to be a liar (about personal things) and saw himself as above everyone around him. He was full of himself and wanted to be treated like a king. He even wanted people to get permission to be in the same room with him. He was not a famous man, though he aspired to be. As I asked God more and more questions on the matter, He led me to the scripture that said God's gifts and calling are without repentance. Romans 11:29 This showed me that God's gifts weren't for perfect people only. God's gifts are a gift. Period. God is true to Himself, true to His word. He remains faithful when we are not faithful. And that is why the gift still functions even if the vessel falls from grace. Our faith should never be in the vessel or their godliness, but in Jesus Christ and His righteousness alone. (Acts 3:12) The vessel will have to give an account at judgement for his choice in how he walked out his calling and used the God given gift.

I was disillusioned with this man and I wasn't sure what to trust for awhile. It was a stepping stone God would use to fill me with wisdom and discernment for things to come.

God then led me to type in healing on YouTube and I found videos put out by Todd White. I watched his street healing videos every free moment for two weeks. There was something about him that felt right. I wound up finding his web site that showed he belonged to a team putting on conferences to teach about what he was doing on the streets. I HAD TO GO! (This was the first year Todd started speaking.) The closest one was in West Virginia. It would be a nine hour drive and only two weeks away. I signed up!

I packed my bag, hugged and kissed my husband and daughters and off I went. I prayed the entire trip down there. The anticipation in me was great! My GPS did a great job of getting me to my hotel. It was August 11th, 2009. I remember the date very well. It too would be a very pivotal day in my choice to follow what I felt God was bringing into my life.

20

I pulled into the hotel parking lot when my phone rang. It was my mom. I parked my car and listened as my mom spoke. She asked me if I was sitting down, I said, "Yes". Right then, I knew--I knew what she was about to say.

"Lisa," she continued, with sadness in her voice, "Your grandfather has just passed away."

My grandfather lived in Florida, another nine hours from where I now was. I was VERY VERY close to my grandfather. Here is the reason why. A few years prior to this, we barely knew each other. I had only seen him a handful of times my entire life. My grandfather had been a hard man. He had lived a life that included violence with a rough nature. Before I was even born, my grandmother left him because of his nature. My mom, along with her brother and sister, feared him.

What happened those years prior to his passing was that God impressed on me to start calling my grandfather every day and tell him that I loved him. He gave no other insight, just, tell him that you love him. So I did. I began to call him every single day. It was awkward at first. But I told him that I loved him and I would prove it by calling him every day and telling him so.

It was amazing to watch the transformation. He was not used to this sort of attention. But day by day, month by month, he grew to expect it. To look forward to it. Then one day, while on one of our calls, his voice got shaky. He said to me, "Why do you call me? Why do you love me? I don't deserve this."

In his heart, he knew he had never been a real part of my life. He had given me no reason to love him so much and shower him with so much attention. I said, "Because I do, Grandpa. I just do, and there is nothing you can do about it."

God knew what He was doing. He knew how to reach my grandfather's heart. To give him a way to experience undeserved, unconditional love and grace. Grace is unmerited love and favor. I didn't fully understand what was going on until everything played itself out by God's great plan.

My grandfather finally grew to understand that God loved him this way too. God's love is undeserved. It's given in spite of us, simply because it is God's nature to forgive and to love. Grandfather had been an agnostic his whole life. Towards the end, through his wife and her family, he grew to believe in Jesus Christ. But that wasn't enough for God. God used me to pursue my grandfather, to free his heavy heart of the burden he had carried for so long, believing he was not worthy of this kind of love. As a result, he now felt the depth of God's love for him. He came to the Lord and was baptized into Christ at age 85. If that weren't enough, to top it off... in those two years before he passed, all relationships with his children were healed and restored. God's word is truth. Love never fails.

Now back to the hotel parking lot in West Virginia. As all these thoughts and memories raced through my mind, I sat in my car and I asked God, "What do I do now?" This scripture popped into my heart, "Let the dead bury the dead, you come and follow Me." Now God wasn't calling my family dead. He knew I would understand what He wanted; He wanted me to stay.

So, I called my family and told them I could not come to bury my grandfather. I didn't want to see him in a casket anyway. I'd much rather remember seeing his face as he came up out of that baptismal water a child of God! I will see him again!

So I stayed--and my life changed!

I made new friends at the Power and Love Conference, and listened to every single word every minister spoke. They didn't just talk the talk, they walked the walk. Healings happened. I saw them! With my own eyes, I saw them! Oh how I wish I could help you feel the excitement and joy I felt after those four days in West Virginia! They showed me things in God's word that blew my mind! I had never seen it that way before. They showed me that Jesus said, "*Anyone who has faith in Me shall do the things I have done and greater things than these.*" John 14:12 (emphasis added) Not just specially anointed ones. They showed me things in scripture about ALL BELIEVERS being able to heal the sick simply because we believe! Jesus said, "These signs will accompany those who have believed: in My name they will cast out demons, they shall speak in new tongues...they will lay hands on the sick, and they will recover. " Mark 16:17. (AMP) I felt both excitement and fear. I had so many teachings and beliefs inside me that didn't match up in my mind because I had been taught that all of that was for the early church. That it was just for the apostles. That it did not carry over to ALL as the bible just said to me. The bible said ANYBODY, it said, ALL. My mind was reeling with this new understanding! However, It would be years yet before my eyes would be opened more fully to see all the traps and boundaries that penned me in, limiting me in my identity. Religion in me ran deep!

In spite of this, I had enough fire from the conferences that I immediately started hitting the streets and praying for strangers. I was scared stiff of talking to strangers! I would literally sit in my car for a good half hour each time I went out trying to get up the nerve to approach people. It wasn't that I didn't believe in what God wanted me to do. It was just that I had NO idea how to start a conversation with a stranger and work it into praying for their healing. But I would do it. And God was so gracious! His Word really was truth, and I started to see healings right away.

It's amazing how after you recognize that God gave you the green light to heal the sick--you see sick people everywhere!!!! I would walk up to people in stores and such and if I saw a wrist brace or knee brace I would ask them what happened, and then pray. God would heal them, but not every time. I think the first year I prayed, I saw maybe 20% get healed. It was just enough to keep me encouraged and pressing into God. I prayed for a lady at the cash register who complained to me that she couldn't hear because she had been sick. She kept touching her ears and doing her best to listen and talk with me. I asked to pray for her and she let me. When I prayed, her ears popped! She said, "My ears just popped--I can hear that guy over there!--I can hear those people over there!!!" She got SO excited! And I had no idea what to do with people after I prayed for them at this point. I was kind of like a sniper who shot them with a gift from God and then left them to deal with what just happened. I started to walk away and this poor lady walked from her cash register and was looking around dumbfounded wanting to tell anyone who would listen what just happened! It was so precious to me and deeply touched my heart. I would ponder these miracle moments for hours and even days afterwards. I was overwhelmed that God was willing to do such things today, through US!

I grew to love praying for cashiers. One was a young girl. She was holding her back, so I asked if she had pain. She said, 'YES!!!" I said, "Watch this! Give me your hand."

She looked at me funny but gave me her hand. I took it and commanded her back to heal and the pain to go in the name of Jesus, then said, "Test it." She moved around, looked at me with "a deer in the headlights look" and said, "Are you an angel?" I laughed and said, "No, not an angel; a child of God. Jesus loves you and wants you to know, He is real."

Then, I sniper modded again and walked away leaving her standing there staring at me, jaw dropped. I would many times go to my truck after these moments, sit in the driver's seat and weep a bit, shaking my head at the amazing awe of God and His love for us all. This was really happening. Just wow!

Other times I would ask to pray for a cashier and they wouldn't have any pain that needed healed physically, so, I would just pray their identity and many times God started to tell me wounds that were in their heart and I would pray healing into that. They would cry and tell me I was right. Some asked how I knew that. But at this stage in my walk, I didn't realize that God was giving me words of knowledge. I didn't realize I was hearing Him speak to my heart. I just thought I got lucky! My heart was so dysfunctional that I didn't believe at this point that God loved me enough to do that kind of stuff through me.

Boundary 2: Hey God--I'm A Woman!

There is no longer Jew or Gentile, slave or free, male and female. For you are all one in Christ Jesus. Galatians 3:28 NLT

It is amazing to me how strong a mindset or stronghold can be. There is a reason why it is called a stronghold. It really does have a strong hold on you. Strongholds are beliefs. Beliefs are a matter of the heart and *"For as he thinks in his heart, so is he."* Psalm 23:7. (NKJV)

All my young life I was told I couldn't do things because I was a girl. Being told that seemed to ignite a fire inside me that said...ya wanna bet! It wasn't feminism. It was just a strong determination to not be limited in who I could be.

In school, I was told trumpets were boys instruments. Girls played flutes and clarinets. My band teacher had enough flutes and clarinets and told me I could pick a trumpet or trombone. I didn't want to carry the trombone home from school so I picked the trumpet. I took on the challenge given me by the boys (that girls can't play as well as boys) and I practiced my horn until I quickly moved into first chair. I kept that chair all through school (minus my freshman and sophomore years in high school, but still played first chair music). I played the national anthem solos at all the basketball games and played taps for memorial day parades. I was in jazz band, pep band, marching band, concert band, you name it. I was known in school for my trumpet playing.

At age 17, I went to a recruiter to join the Army. I've always been a bit of a tomboy and liked being strong physically. The recruiter and I became good friends. He would come visit me at my house after our visits at his office. He said I was one tough cookie and he liked me. The reason why was because of a half hour conversation where I argued with him about what they should let women be in the service. My first choice was to be a paratrooper. He said, "No, you'll need to pick something else. That is a front line position and we don't put women there." I argued that I was just as fast and could shoot a gun just as good as any man. He smiled and tried to talk me into being a nurse. That would be as close to the front-line as he could get me. I responded, "Not happening; then let me be a sniper." He smiled again and said, "Front line; can't do it." I argued my case a bit longer and then said, "OK then I want to be an MP! (Military Police)" He laughed out loud this time and said, "You are a stubborn thing arn't you!" He looked through his book and read that the requirements were that a woman had to be 5' 3" and at least 105lbs. So I made him weigh me and check my height. I was 5' 3" and 102lbs. I told him I could gain the weight in muscle at boot camp. He said, "What are you going to do when a 200lb man says no to you when you tell him to do something?" I said, "I'll shoot him!" (I wouldn't have really...but I wanted to sound tough enough to get in.) He belly laughed and was really nice to me, but said no to all my requests.

So, this was an epic fail for me, and all because I was born a girl! This sort of thing happened all through my life. It caused me to get tougher and stronger emotionally and physically, but was also a great frustration.

***

Next, here I was with the bible and I was seeing it all over again. In the various churches I grew up in, a woman had no other value in the church than to feed guests, teach Sunday school to kids and sit in the daycare as a church nanny.

27

It was because of this, along with many wrongful interpretations of scriptures pertaining to women; and the fact that women in the bible were not really talked about in any detail in church which would encourage women to be amazing that I had a grudge against God. I felt He was unfair and a bigot (just being real). To be honest, I felt devalued and of lower worth than a man. This wound created a resentment in me that ran deep. I didn't want to be better than a man, just thought of as equal. Equal in value and worth with better options than what I saw were available.

After seeing Maria Woodworth-Etter and Katherine Kuhlman being used by God the way He did, it really made me ask God a lot of questions. It took *much* time and many many people to convince me that women could be used by God in such ways. That it was actually OK with God.

God then led me to read stories in the bible itself about women such as Deborah--Deborah was a prophet of God! She was a female Judge! She was a warrior who led an army! Judges CH 4-5. Then there was Huldah who was also a prophetess and advisor to the king of Judah. 2 Kings 22.

In Luke 2:36-38 it talks about a New Testament Prophetess named Anna who had dedicated her life to the Lord worshipping night and day, fasting and praying. God honored her by allowing her to see the Lord Jesus face to face and prophecy about Him to all who were looking forward to the redemption of Jerusalem. What an amazing honor! God loved her and used her even in her old age!

God gave wisdom and boldness to Ester. He guarded and guided her life in such a way that she changed the course of history. Ester convinced an entire nation of people to fast and pray for three days. As a result of her love for God and her people, God moved in tremendous power swaying the thoughts of the King and thus saving her people.

Then there was the evidence I was seeing in my own walk. God was confirming His word through me! I had been shown by God that while my church did not accept what God was doing through me, I was free to "go into all the world and preach the gospel to all creation!" Mark 16:15 which led to Mark 16:16-17 which reads: *These signs will accompany those who have believed: in My name they will cast out demons, they will speak with new tongues; they will pick up serpents, and if they drink any deadly poison, it will not hurt them; they will lay hands on the sick, and they will recover.*

Then the disciples went out and preached everywhere, and the Lord worked with them and confirmed his word by the signs that accompanied it. Mark 16:20 NIV

"I tell you the truth, anyone who believes in me will do the same works I have done, and even greater works, because I am going to be with the Father. John 14:12 NLT

I put these here because I want you to see what God showed me. In Mark 16:20 it says "the disciples". In John 14:12 it says, "I tell you the truth, "anyone"... In Mark 16:17 it says, "those who believe". This meant ME! This means YOU!

The Lord will confirm His word by signs and wonders for ALL who believe in Him and follow Him. He went on to say He would work WITH them to confirm His word and they will do the <u>same</u> works that Jesus did! Glory! What a profound revelation for someone like me who was so deep in fear that I would be doing something against God's will or desires for me, a woman.

My desire for you, dear reader, is that you lay out your questions and desires before God with your whole heart. He listens! Persevere and never give up in your searching for truth. The truth will come! And when it does, "The truth will set you free!"

***

Father, bless the one reading this today. Give them hope. In Jesus' name, I pray for them to be consumed with hunger to know You better; to understand Your word for them as an individual; that You would have written the whole bible just for them--a love letter full of treasures just waiting for them to find and ignite dreams, desires and hope for a fresh experience in this life hand in hand with You their Father in Heaven. Come Holy Spirit and council, comfort and set ablaze Your child, for the glory of God and His Son Jesus Christ. Jesus--You deserve our love! I thank you Lord, in Jesus' name, So be it.
God's peace to you...

Boundary 3 : Sins Disqualified me.
The lie...I'm going to hell

Therefore, there is now no condemnation for those who are in Christ Jesus. Roman 8:1 NIV

My past sins were a powerful boundary for me. Sin and what we believe about our own sin is a game changer. It can destroy your life and keep you in incredible bondage if you don't understand scripture (what it says about your freedom from sin in Christ), and/or have a wrong perception of God (Is He a kind, merciful, forgiving God? Or is He scrutinizing, harsh and distant). I had both a wrong understanding of scripture and a wrong view of God.

What I am about to share with you is one of *the* main catalysts in making me who I am today. The transition from feeling damned because of my sins as a Christian (a works mentality, meaning you have to work by being good to earn God's love and right standing), into understanding my freedom in Christ and His righteousness. It's amazing how you can go to churches your whole life and still not understand who God really is. I've learned that much of this confusion comes because of the flaws of those teaching God's word and of those who profess to believe in it. Some of the churches I went to taught a very legalistic way of going--that Christians had to walk out a very tight line, a very strict path, and while they professed that God loved you-- they also professed that if you sin, you will go to hell. I learned that people teach from their own views of their own lives--what is in their hearts. If they are judgmental people who live both judging others and themselves harshly, then they teach this attribute into the person of God. It is how they see Him and feel seen by Him.

Before my clarity came, I believed in a harsh God who punished sin in the Christian. As a result, I suffered pain night after night in deepest despair because of a raging war that was going on inside of me. One part of me was so on fire and desiring to do many wonderful works for God (such as praying for the sick believing for a miracle), the other side equally powerful in saying-- "You are not qualified! You are the worst of sinners, and Lisa--you are going to hell no matter what you do for God going forward."

Do you remember the story in Matthew 19 where the rich man wanted to know, "What good deed must I do to have eternal life?" Jesus said, "Why ask me about what is good? There is only One who is good. But to answer your question--if you want to receive eternal life, keep the commandments." "Which one's?" the man asked. And Jesus replied: "'You must not murder. You must not commit adultery. You must not steal. You must not testify falsely. Honor your father and mother. Love your neighbor as yourself.'"
"I've obeyed all these commandments," the young man replied. "What else must I do?" Jesus told him: "If you want to be perfect, go and sell all your possessions and give the money to the poor, and you will have treasure in heaven. Then come, follow me."

When I look at the whole of my life on this earth, in some way or form, I have broken all of them. I didn't physically murder anyone; but Jesus teaches that if we hate our brother, it is the same as murder. And before I got to where I am now...I hated some folks and wished they were dead. Just being real. My heart hadn't been healed by love yet.

In that season of my life journey, I had a twisted view of scriptures. I had believed that the bible said, God forgave confessed sins; however, I didn't 'feel' forgiven. The bible taught that God forgets our sins. But I didn't have a grid for that. How could He forget them if I constantly remembered them? He is God. He knows everything. I lived a very sin conscious life. I felt that God was always scrutinizing me for *every* thought, feeling and action. It was overwhelming at times. Have you ever felt that way?

I know the truth now, but I need to share the journey as it was, so that hopefully my journey will speak to someone else and bring freedom from the lies.

So, here we go. Not only had I been a hypocrite Christian most of my young life--meaning, I professed to love God, put on the mask of being a good person and so on, but my actions were less than holy. The temptations of the world were still able to speak loudly to me because I didn't comprehend yet just how much God loved me (more on that in the next chapter). There came a day in my Christian journey where a weakness showed up in my heart and the temptations in this life overcame me. I wanted to go back to the world and do what I wanted to do without feeling condemnation. I wanted free from His all seeing eye and felt I could just tune Him out and live my life away from the constant judgment. The conversation went something like this: "God, I can't feel you, I can't see you, and I can't hear you. *You are not real enough!* So, I want you to just go away! Leave me alone. I choose hell over you!"

I didn't stop believing in God. I KNEW He existed. I didn't renounce my faith. I just wanted Him to go away and leave me alone so I could enjoy myself. The world and sin had its pleasures that gave immediate gratification. God seemed very distant to me and the rewards of heaven too far off. This lasted about three months. Now this is where I felt really shameful. During those three months. I felt free! Free from God's ever-prying eye. I was doing my best to live like He didn't exist. It's kinda like the kid who hides under a blanket and thinks no one can see them. You stole a cookie and think no one knows about it. Or like the teenager who is on a trip far from home, far from mom and dad and they feel this freedom from the rules of home and can do what they wish. It was kinda like that. Problem is--eventually, you've gotta come home and give an account for what you've been up to. So that freedom feeling was fleeting. Eventually, fear set in.

I tried my best to tune God out. Putting my fingers in my spiritual ears crying la-la-la-la-la. But, for complaining that I couldn't hear God--He sure was being LOUD in convicting me and trying to draw me back! I wish I could have understood then what I understand now. God was my Father and like any loving Father, He was yelling to me, STOP! YOU'RE IN DANGER! Just as your earthly father would if you were about to run across a five lane interstate with traffic flying by at 70 miles an hour. "Come back to Me! It's safe over here with Me!" He was crying out.

I did come back. Not because I saw Him as my loving Father, but because I had developed a fear of the Lord that caused me to see just where I was and that I needed to change quickly. I hated who I was and what I had become. But--how could God forgive me now? I told Him flat out, "I choose the world and what it offers over You! I choose hell over You." And then I willfully sinned against Him.

Did you know that Satan is still the same now as he was in the garden? His favorite tactic to keep you in bondage and separated from God. is to use God's words and twist them into a meaning other than what God intended them for. When you don't know God's true nature and heart, you will easily believe a lie.

After I came back, I began searching the scriptures to see if God would forgive me for my willful disobedience. So many scriptures seemed to say that He would. But then I found this passage which reads: *26If we deliberately keep on sinning after we have received the knowledge of the truth, no sacrifice for sins is left,27but only a fearful expectation of judgment and of raging fire that will consume the enemies of God. 28Anyone who rejected the law of Moses died without mercy on the testimony of two or three witnesses. 29How much more severely do you think someone deserves to be punished who has trampled the Son of God underfoot, who has treated as an unholy thing the blood of the covenant that sanctified them, and who has insulted the Spirit of grace? 30For we know him who said, "It is mine to avenge; I will repay," and again, "The Lord will judge his people." 31It is a dreadful thing to fall into the hands of the living God. Hebrews 10:26- 31*

The devil had me completely consumed in fear that all my life, I had known of Jesus and His sacrifice for me and yet all my life, I willfully sinned, or as this passage read--kept on deliberately sinning and therefore, there was no longer any sacrifice for sin for me. I had trampled on the blood of Jesus and spat on His grace over and over and over again.

There was a point when this so consumed me that I cried myself to sleep nearly every night for two years. No one knew it but God. During the day, I would put on my "happy" face and walk out my day as if all was well with me and the world. But every night--I saw my future in hell.

I can remember one night that I was laying in bed praying before God and I was crying so hard. I felt like God didn't love me, that my life was a lie and I was a lost cause. I can't remember all the details leading up to this moment, but what I do remember is that I was laying there praying believing that God was far from me when I had a vision. I saw God standing in front of me and He took one step backwards-- only one step. But in the moment that He did that, it felt like all life left me and I was in a black hole. The black was penetrating and deep and heavy. In that moment I couldn't feel anything, I couldn't see anything. It was as if life stopped. It was a place of emptiness, absolute emptiness. There was no hope, no future, no past. It was like a vacuum sucked everything out of me and it was an absolute void. I started to panic and great fear gripped my heart. As soon as I got that afraid, I saw God step back forward and peace came over me. God spoke to my spirit and said, "I have never left you nor forsaken you." I began sobbing and sobbing. Because I came to the realization that even when I thought God was not near me, all through my life that He was always near me. That if He had taken even one step away, life would have been completely different. It was never Him moving away from me because of my sin, it was me moving away from Him and creating boundaries and barriers.

God is love.

As we continue through the boundaries you will begin to notice something. Each boundary is a trap of the mind. Once truth comes in--you are free.

Belief is powerful.

What you believe is what controls what you think, what you feel and how you will walk out your life. It's a matter of the heart. What is trapped inside there?

Let's continue…

It wasn't long after this that God explained to me that I was not being held to what I read in Hebrews 10. That He always forgives the repentant heart. Jesus paid for every single sin. I had not blasphemed the Holy Spirit (which is the ONLY unpardonable sin) I had simply not grown into the fullness of truth yet. The truth that He loved me, and He wanted me to walk in the freedom He paid for more than I did. I argued with Him about this for quite some time. I really felt that I fit the description in that verse. But what that verse was talking about, was the one who knew Christ, had received the knowledge of truth and then chose to no longer believe in Him as their Lord and Savior. They had chosen to not believe in their salvation through Jesus Christ. God explained to me that I had not done that. I had simply been a child full of questions and misconceptions. I fell. But He was always ready to receive me and pick me back up as soon as I was ready.

I wish I could tell you that this knowledge of truth fixed me. Sadly, I continued to struggle, holding myself accountable to my past sins with much less mercy than God did for some time longer. Old mindsets can be hard to let go of.

Interestingly, something remarkable began to take place though, I began to recognize that I truly could hear God. He had always been there guiding me all through my life. I just didn't trust it was Him. I thought it was arrogant to think I was actually hearing God. I felt so worthless and unworthy of such a thing. It was a beautiful thing to discover that He loved me that much and wanted to communicate with me.

(For all who are led by the Spirit of God are sons of God. Romans 8:14 BSB) After I reconnected to God and chose to give Him my whole life, I began a journey of learning new ways to hear his voice. I share more on that in Boundary 10.

Recognizing that I could hear Him was only the beginning. He was about to get bigger and bigger and bigger, shattering box after box after box that I had shrunk Him down and put Him in through wrong religious beliefs. I began to experience God in tangible ways. I began feeling His power go through my body when praying for others. Feeling that same power coming from others into me. Feeling His anointing in powerful ways on my person while I prayed for others and much much more. So, when I had formerly complained that I could not hear God, could not feel Him, that He wasn't real enough for me--that changed *dramatically* from that season forward.

I was about to learn just how alive, interactive and powerful God is. It simply required faith!

In conclusion, God, by His Holy Spirit, taught me that though I was imperfect in so many ways--my sins had not disqualified me. *My faith in Jesus qualified me.* My righteousness is found in Him alone. It is not by my works that I am qualified. Nor by my sins that I am disqualified. At least not in God's eyes. Man may judge you harshly and disqualify you for things. Just being born a woman caused men to disqualify me for things in the beginning. But I would learn that only my faith in Jesus made me pure in God's eyes. It was my faith in Him, NOT my faith in *me*, that made all things possible. Thank you, Jesus!

***

Father, I pray for anyone who has felt disqualified to serve you because of their past. Cleanse them now Lord and help them to see that it is by faith in You that we are made righteous and whole. Our trust is in You. Our hope is in You, and our power and abilities are found in You. Set this captive free from fear that they are not good enough to serve You in power and gifting. If they feel disqualified, show them that in Jesus they are fully qualified as our righteousness is found in You. In Jesus' name. Amen

If you are still dealing with a sin friend, repent and turn back to God. He LOVES you and His forgiveness is immediate and complete. Do yourself a great favor by turning completely to God in all things. There is nothing as good in this world as walking out your life with a clean heart before God. His peace is waiting for you. Once you have found this peace--go--and give it to others near you. Bless you on your journey.

Boundary 4: Fear Of Man

But made himself of no reputation, and took upon him the form of a servant, and was made in the likeness of men. Philippians 2:7 KJV

It's amazing to me how God will bring something to the surface about you that you didn't grasp you had. I knew I had rejection issues--but I didn't grasp that the majority of that issue stemmed from needing to have a reputation. I thought it was normal for us all to develop our reputations. That's the way the world works. Whoever had the best reputation before others was exalted, was looked up to, was popular, was accepted by all and esteemed by all.

It all started way back in elementary school when we learned there were popular kids and unpopular kids. There were awards for being the best at things. Nearly everything we did was a contest. Getting graded on our work, you were either the smart kid or the dumb kid. You were the best at sports or you were a nerd. We were labeled. And everyone desired to advance themselves to be awarded and held in high esteem starting at a very young age.

As we grew up, it transferred into adult life as well. We were shown through the media that the people who got celebrated were those who made the most money, had the highest position in their workplace or was extremely talented at something being better than everyone else. And so, I was no different.

When I was thirteen, I began training dogs and I had no idea at the time the journey that would take me on. I had a miniature schnauzer at the time, and our little town knew me as the girl with the well trained dog. I got involved in 4-H and when the fair came, I entered myself and my dog in both showmanship and obedience classes. I won everything! First place in my classes and Grand Champion overall. The newspaper came and took our photos, and I instantly became famous.

Wow! MY picture was right there, great big in our local paper. I felt so special. I had found what I was good at, so I continued to work with dogs moving forward. At 16 years old, I was teaching dog obedience classes to grown ups. This again boosted my ego and made me feel important.

As time went on, I would eventually marry at age 25. We bought our own 5-acre farm and my husband said, "I've always wanted a Rottweiler." Well, say no more! Me being an animal lover deluxe, I ran right out and bought him a little female for Christmas. He loved her! But chimed in again and said, "A female is nice, but I had always wanted a male." Well, say no more--Off I went and bought us a nice strong male puppy and there we were--Rottweiler owners.

I fell in love with the breed, started showing our male in obedience trials and did well. I started meeting new people and got involved showing them in both AKC/UKC and german-style confirmation shows. I also trained and competed in Schutzhund, weight pulling, endurance running, obedience trials and tracking trials. I got deeply enmeshed in the breed and competing. Most of my dogs were imported from all over the world as I had to have the best I could find. I became a well known breeder who received top dollar for my puppies having a waiting list for my litters. Major rottweiler breed magazines hosted articles and many photos of my dogs and me. People knew who I was and that I brought competition.

I ate, drank, dreamt and slept being the best with my breed. I studied bloodlines, I knew what everyone else had in their kennels. I understood phenotypes and temperaments and knew which lines did what and how they produced. I had become a master of my trade.

I had a reputation.

After 22 years of that, my life began going in a new direction. God had called me out and wanted me to let go of it all. It was time to focus my attention on Him.

***

I find it interesting that the fear of rejection for doing what you love in the world feels different than the fear of rejection we feel for sharing our faith in Jesus Christ. Especially if you are walking out your faith by believing Jesus will move in power to cast out a devil, to heal someone or to share that you are hearing from God prophetically. There is definitely a spiritual amplification to create a fear of loss or the possibility of hostility towards you.

I now found myself struggling to build a new reputation.

God is patient...

It's amazing, being on this end of things now, looking back and seeing just how patient He really is-- how He allows us to muddle through many many experiences in life if need be to help us to finally and clearly understand what's happening and why we can't find our peace.

Needing to maintain a reputation creates fear of man. It creates fear of rejection of those in your circle--fear of being demoted, devalued, disagreed with and dejected.

God put the call in my heart in 2006 to believe for greater things. In 2009 I got accelerated into walking it out and began sharing it by openly giving testimonies. It was at this time that God would begin the journey of revelation to my heart that I was trapped in a lie which said I needed to create and maintain a reputation.

Others in the faith whom I esteemed seemed to have a great reputation in the Lord. I thought in order for me to feel like I had any value as a person in the faith, that I would need to somehow develop a great reputation in the faith as well.

This owned me.

I was owned by the need for people to love me and accept me--for God to love me and accept me. (Keep in mind that all the boundaries presented in this book were present from the beginning. I was learning to overcome them all collectively). I feared being rejected, and this is the fear of man.

Going through this journey with God was emotional for me. I had to work hard to overcome all the fear. Fear kept me unproductive. Was what I was experiencing in this season real and from God? Was it really OK? Meaning, was it all of

God (Hearing God prophetically, seeing people healed instantly, manifestations of both the demonic and angelic)? I had no teacher within my church to help me understand. No one in church taught how to hear and discern God's voice. Which voice was God? Which was my own? Which was from the devil? Oh, how often I cried to God for discernment and to not be led into deception! "Guard my heart and protect me Lord" was my constant cry.

Everything God was leading me to do was producing great fruit. But I was still battling with my past teaching of these things not being for today. Your mind is powerful. I felt like I was in a constant war in how to live my life. Everything inside me wanted to see the power of God moving today to set people free via healing and prophetic encouragement, yet I feared how others would receive this new me. You see, the church I attended did not do any of these things. As a matter of fact, they brushed past the spiritual gifts and claimed that the great power moves that were seen with the apostles died with the apostles. But I had called out to the Lord in my private prayer time for truth about it all. "God," I said, "Are you the same yesterday, today and forever? And if so, where is your power today?" And so He began to teach me.

Now, this woman (me) who had attended this church, growing up in it, was very different than the leadership once knew. I went from being the normal church attender who sat and listened in the pews each Sunday, to being a Spirit-filled street evangelist who saw radical results. Many being instant results that could be verified. (And they had not taught me this! I learned this from sitting alone for countless hours in the presence of God, being led and taught by His Spirit.) This caused the leadership to have many meetings because of me. They knew me and loved me. So, how were they going to deal with me now? I battled the fear of man-- wanting my church family to continue to love and accept me, (I was now treated like the black sheep of the family. They loved me, but would not celebrate me, and one elder in

44

particular flat out hated the new me and confronted me with his anger). Yet, I had an even greater love of God and what He was willing to do with us and through us as His children. Therefore I could not stop; but advance.

My testimony is truly a testament to the power of God to transform, as the truth in his Word became the living reality of my life.

It is *because* He was so real now, *because* His miracles were happening before my eyes, *because* His Word was becoming so active and real in my life, that it gave me the power to endure the rejection of those I esteemed around me (the leaders of my church, the church congregation, friends and family, strangers on the street). It was all new to all of them as well, so I was constantly trying to convince them that what I was experiencing was real. In this process I was experiencing their rejection, their questions, their concerns about me. AND, all the while I am working towards convincing them of the reality of this new amazing experience of my life, I was full of questions myself. My brain, my thoughts bombarded me daily with-- is this really real? Are these people really getting healed? Are they being honest when they say that they have been? Even with the proof they provided me, it shook me at my core that the God I had learned about in the Bible really *was* alive and more real than I had capacity (at the time) to believe before. He was no longer a story I was expected to believe as truth. He was revealing Himself as the living God, active and interactive with His children in Christ today!

It's amazing to me how the mind works--that you can see people before your eyes getting healed and yet when you go home, your rational mind, your carnal mind, will find every reason why it couldn't have happened and that it wasn't real. And yet the people kept coming to me with joyful faces and would tell me how wonderfully God had in fact healed them. Some came with documentation from their Doctors.

I needed to see that documentation as much as anybody in the beginning. I was going through a tremendous paradigm shift at the power I now witnessed that came from belief and faith in the truth of God's word through *us!*

I desperately want to explain my journey with you because I think I was the most messed up person on the planet for God to choose for this. I was messed up emotionally and struggled violently against what He was trying to teach me; what He was trying to teach me about Himself, about the truth of His word, about His love for me and for you, and that I was safe with Him. I had never felt safe with God. But I share that in yet another part of this book.

***

The Depression

I kept questioning God, "Why am I so depressed all the time? Why can't I get free from this never-ending cycle of depression?" I had been living my life literally on what would look like a roller coaster, where I would be on a great high and enjoying life, to where I would find myself in strong depression with suicidal thoughts. This just didn't make sense. Why should a Christian who has the love of Jesus Christ and is seeing God move through great signs and wonders have the ability to fall into depression the way I was doing so consistently? I was declaring freedom over everyone around me and yet I was not living in the freedom myself. None of my friends seem to be able to help me. They would pray for me, console me, edify me, encourage me and tell me how much God loves me, and yet the cycle continued. Then there came a day while I was reading my Bible that I came across a passage where it spoke of Jesus being a man of *no reputation.*

REPUTATION.

The word jumped off the page.

I got stuck on the passage where Jesus spoke of not accepting the judgments of men. He only accepted God's word over Himself. And then there was Paul who also declared such things. That he did not receive the judgments of men because men's hearts were imperfect and that he didn't even judge his own heart because only God knows the true motives of the heart. And something clicked.

As I meditated on this further, I began to see that God was healing my heart of the boundary of having a reputation and that my grief and pride came from the need to have a reputation. God was showing me that it was time to let go of man's interpretations of me. They all see me through their own heart lenses and therefore cannot judge me correctly. No, I cannot even judge myself correctly. Only God can truly judge my heart knowing what my true motives are. I learned that I was in deception. And through this revelation, God showed me that deception keeps you from seeing a truth. Because you cannot tell that you are in deception or believing a lie while you are trapped in the lie, you yourself cannot truly judge your own heart.

I had been living my life for other people's opinions of me.

When you live your life allowing other people to dictate your happiness, by whether they accept you or reject you, they own you.

You will live every day of your life looking for that acceptance from them. You will modify your behavior in order to gain that acceptance and to feel valuable in their eyes. I had been doing this my whole life. I had been modifying my behavior depending on the person I was standing in front of in hope of gaining acceptance and feeling valuable in their eyes.
This caused great conflict in me because I felt the draw from God to walk out my life in a way that would cause others to reject me. It took me 10 years of fighting against this type of rejection, constantly going into states of depression, *to finally get so tired of it that I saw the need to accept something new.* The new thing that I needed to accept, was the truth that God loves me and that I am safe in that love--that it was OK for imperfect people to reject me as long as I understood I was accepted by God. At this point, I had finally grown to the point of knowing that this was true of God. That if the entire world rejected me and turned their backs on me, that God would be enough.

I worked very hard to grow into having a pure heart before God where I feel no condemnation. And my relationship with God is such that, if I get off course in any way at all, He tells me, we work through it, and we continue on. But even when He chastises me, He is so-o-o-o-o kind and patient. I never feel He is angry with me; just leading me. This was so so huge for me. Because I hadn't believed that God loved me my whole life. I felt dirty, tarnished by sin and my lack of ability to abstain from it.

I discovered why it was so hard to abstain from sinning. You will sin when you don't understand just how deeply loved you are by God. When you don't feel complete in Him or satisfied or content. When you don't feel perfect love from Him, you expect punishment from Him. You will find yourself unable to behave in any other way than to do things that deserve punishment. But when you finally grasp the intensity of God's love for you--that He is for you and not against you, that He wants the best for you, that He is always seeking for your good, you yourself will fall in love with the One who first loved you. It will break your heart, causing you great sorrow to do *anything* that would break His heart or cause separation from this perfect love.

I thought my whole life that I was pursuing God, trying to get Him to see me and accept me. It wasn't until my friend, Joel Sweeney, told me to stop pursuing God that this changed. Joel said, "I want you to run from God. I want you to stop praying, stop worshiping, stop reading your bible. Just live your life as if He doesn't exist for a few weeks and let God pursue you." I didn't realize just how badly I was trapped in a works mentality to gain God's love, approval and acceptance until I was asked to do this seemingly simple thing.

I got off the phone with Joel and I sobbed and sobbed and sobbed, because I didn't believe that God would pursue me. I thought if I didn't do all the religious acts that had been drummed into me my whole life, as to what a good Christian was supposed to do to please God, that He would drop me like a hot coal. It was all I knew. It was all I did, every day. I had lived a life of begging God to love me. Everyday I begged Him to forgive every little thing I saw in myself that I felt fell short of perfection. I was a hot mess! I needed to have a reputation with God! But Joel had an INCREDIBLE relationship with Jesus unlike any I had ever witnessed, so I trusted him and did what he asked.

I found it very difficult to try to ignore God and just do what came each day. But God--He must have smiled so big at my obedience to this challenge because He started doing things to show me how He was in fact pursuing ME! He wanted to show me how much He loved me. He just needed me to get out of the way, to stop living in fear, and believe that He loved me more than I love myself.

49

This began a new season in my life where I began to see the power of pursuit of God in my life on a consistent and continual basis. God was in overdrive revealing Himself as all sufficient. That He heard me and knew the cries of my heart. He began showing His love for me by fulfilling my needs that no one knew about. Needs that I kept in my heart alone--but He knew. This was indisputable love from Him that I could not deny.

As He continued to do this over the next two years, answering my prayers in ways that boggled my mind, I developed a love and security in Him that helped me to see that *the ONLY reputation that I needed or wanted to have, was my clear conscience before God.* I have a clear conscience because I live in abiding never ceasing prayer with Him. We talk all day every day. I wake up thinking about Him and I go to bed thinking about Him. He wakes me in the middle of the night and my first thoughts are of Him.

You can't fully love someone until you feel fully loved yourself. You can't fully love someone until you no longer need them to return that love back to you to fulfill a need in you.

Because I feel fully loved and accepted by God, I was able to learn to fully love myself, and because I now love myself (accept myself as I am, faults and all, resting in God's love), I'm free to love others without putting an expectation of a return of that love. Jesus loved all, and sacrificed Himself as an eternal act of love all the while those He loved were crucifying Him.

It's amazing, I am never depressed anymore. I discovered that the depression came because I needed the approval of others. When you give up the need to have a reputation, you take away the power of others to dictate your value. The judgements of others no longer have power. Their words may sting in the moment, but they will not cling to you.

All human judgements are imperfect.

People can only see a very small portion of who you are. No one has seen everything in your life to understand why you do what you do or what led up to it. They are judging, many times, through their own brokenness and faulty perceptions of truth. Only God's judgements are pure. Only God sees all and knows all (even better than we can see ourselves). Only God sees you from perfection in pure love.

There is an extraordinary peace and joy in life when you set yourself free, not only from the fear of the judgements of others, but from your OWN self judgements. God was teaching me to rely ONLY on His judgements of me; and I feel safe with Him.

Now this does not mean that I never listen to criticism from people. I am actually very open to people sharing if they see something wrong in me. But the difference is, I listen for the heart of God in them. If they are speaking from any other place, I just give it to God and ask Him to let me know if He sees anything He wants to touch in me. Other times, I can instantly recognize the person is speaking from the heart of God, and I will go before the Lord for further instruction in my prayer time.

Not only do I walk in an amazing freedom from judgement or rejection, I am also very hard to offend. It still happens occasionally, but it lasts only a brief moment and it's gone. Why? Because God has helped me to understand that if a person's behavior does not reflect the fruit of the Spirit, which are; love, joy, peace, patience, kindness, goodness, faithfulness, gentleness and self-control, they are broken and need God's love in that area of their life. This goes for me too! It is the standard by which I judge my own thoughts, words and actions.

When you can see that someone is broken, your response should be to bless them. So, if someone goes off on you in anger (and you had only acted in true love) you can see they need more of God's healing in their own lives so that they are able to walk in love, joy, peace, patience, kindness, goodness, faithfulness, gentleness and self-control. They need more of God's Spirit active in their life. They need Jesus! It's hard to get offended when you see them through that lens. This is another reason why God said, "bless those that curse you, pray for those who despitefully use you." Luke 6:28

Did you know you can't hate someone you are blessing? It's not possible. Try this test. Smile right now and try to hate someone. You can not smile a genuine heartfelt smile and hate at the same time.

Now, pray blessings (really good blessings) over someone you are holding anger in your heart towards. You will feel your heart soften as you are praying. Pray like this; Father I want to thank you for this opportunity to come to you for my friend _____. I'm asking that you heal every brokenness within them. Help them to know you, to experience your love and to experience your peace. I bless their family, their job, their property and belongings. I bless their health and well-being. I pray that you heal us both and set us free from all the works of the enemy. Release us from anger, bitterness, selfishness and unforgiveness. Help us to walk undivided as one body in Christ Jesus. Thank you for answering my prayer as it is in your will and the desire of your heart. In Jesus' name, Amen.

God is healing YOU by having you do this. It may be hard to say, 'my friend'. But if you do, it will change your heart.

***

The next thing that is important to share here is that not only will other people's criticism of who you are, what you do or what you believe, have less impact on your heart, but the same is to be said of praise and adoration.

Just as a person cannot judge me perfectly to say I am not up to their standards in (fill in the blank), I understand that when people tell me I'm a good person, or I'm amazing, or they share things that make me feel adored, I know they don't know me perfectly, because if they did, they may not say such grand things.

Just because I did a good thing or said something that blessed someone or prayed and saw someone healed doesn't make me good. Even the Lord Jesus said, "Why do you call me good? No one is good except God alone." Mark 10:18. If you see good in me, you know it originated with God, and He is the one deserving of the glory. Knowing this, really helps to keep one humble.

Part of my issue that caused me so much depression was the need to be seen as good. The freedom came when I stopped living for others acceptance and approval and just loved them free grata. This was the most frightening thing I had ever been asked to do in my life--trust God to love me so much that I was willing to let go of the outcome of my life. Meaning, let go of who got to be in my life and who could not be a part of my life. I let go of the direction my life would take and gave it to God. I learned to trust that God knew what I needed better than I knew what I needed. I needed to learn that I could live without things or people I felt I could not live without. Not realizing that they were idols. Anything or anyone you feel you cannot live without, owns you, *and you will serve it in order to keep it.* Only God gets to have that position. So, in this process of learning to live without a reputation--removing the power of people to dictate whether or not I had a good day or a bad day emotionally--I also learned to live my life with my hands held open. God got to choose what He put into my hands/life or what He wanted to take out of my hands/life. I was very fear-filled going into this level of trust in the beginning. Everyday--I would say out loud: "I trust you. I trust you, God. I trust you."

Time would pass and as I left my life in God's hands in this way, He has proven to me that I can in fact trust Him with the whole of my life and all that I am. It sets me free from endless concerns or worries. I now live my life moment to moment as He leads, and it is good.

***

The next step in my freedom from the power of others over my emotions was, that God spent a lot of time teaching me the concept of loving without condition.

People can tell when you want something from them. When you want something from somebody, it can cause them to feel that you are draining them or taking something from them they may not want to give. Therefore, they resist what you are offering, even if it is a good thing (because the motive at its root is self-centered--you want a return on your investment). BUT, when you begin to do things for others without the expectation of getting anything in return, they will want you around because you give life to them. You are a giver, not a taker. And, because you are there solely to love and bless them, they feel the *freedom* to love and bless you back.

How often do you say I love you to someone because deep down you long to hear them say, I love you too. This is selfish. It isn't freely given. It is offered with an expectation of a return. If it is not returned, you then feel offended in your heart. You feel unloved. You feel like you just put yourselves out there only to get hurt. So next time, you withhold love. You say to yourself, they didn't return love to me so I am not going to show it back to them. This is not love. It is manipulation at best and emotional control at worst.

I used to be that person. I would become vulnerable and tell people that I loved them and when I didn't get the response I hoped for, I was shattered and felt the pain of it for a very long time. This at times had the power to cause bitterness, resentment, unforgiveness and a host of other ugly things.

However, when God taught me about the freedom of unconditional love, I found extreme freedom and peace. I was only able to do this though, after I knew my security in God's love for me. When I understood His *unconditional* love for me, I was able to live that out towards others. Every heart desires this kind of love. To be cherished, valued, to feel protected, safe and pursued as someone of great worth, to have someone who sees every part of you, the good and the bad and still wants you and to love you deeply. Every heart deep inside, desires Jesus.

Interesting fact

I discovered that people can take nearly everything away from me in this life, but the one thing NO ONE has control over, is who I choose to love. You can hate me and do all kinds of evil against me, but I can still choose to love you and there is nothing you can do about it. Love or hate is a choice. The initial feeling or emotion you experience might not be in your control, but what you choose to do after that moment is a choice.

God gave me homework to do until this truth settled deep within my heart. He had me love people who hated me, with no expectation of them ever loving me back. He had me do that by praying incredible, powerful prayers over them and their lives. He said to pray prayers over them that you wish someone who loved you would pray over you. He showed me his word that said,

"...bless those who curse you, and pray for those who despitefully use you. Luke 6:28

But I tell you, love your enemies and pray for those who persecute you. Matt 5:44

I began to do just that and it healed my heart. Those who hated me no longer had power to hurt my heart. I had made a decision that no matter what they did, my response would be to bless them and love them. And it was genuine.

This then grew into stage two. God then had me release any thought or idea that I should even expect a thank you from a good deed done. As a matter of fact, He wanted me to search for ways to bless people without them ever finding out it was me. My giving was to be before God alone. My thanks--from Him. My reward--knowing that in that moment I got to look like Him.

By learning to give love freely in the many ways God would teach me, with no expectation of that love being returned, I found that I was FREE! Your feelings can't get hurt if you give a gift to simply give a gift. Your feelings can't get hurt if you pour out all you have to bless another for free, with no expectations of a return on the investment. It is absolutely liberating! I no longer judged their love for me by whether they gave a gift back or said thank you. I chose to do it all from my heart. Free love. I no longer sat around judging others trying to figure out why they treated me the way they did. I no longer had the fear of man. Fear of man lost its power over my life. I chose to live a life of no reputation.

***

If you are like me, in the beginning, I would tell God, "But what about me, I have needs too ya know?" This is where trust had to take root. God has a principle in his word that says that what a man sows he shall reap. In the beginning, you will feel like you are suffering loss. You plant seeds in your garden day and night. You watch them go into the ground and disappear. Then nothing happens for a long time. Or so it seems. But slowly, in time, things begin to grow and grow. Until one day, a harvest much larger than what you planted is poured into your lap.

It's a law--give and you shall receive. Check out Luke 6:38.

To recap: To become free from the boundary of the fear of man, give up your desire to have a reputation. Just be you with a heart that feels no condemnation before God. If you are off track, He will put a check in your spirit. Live clean before Him and be led by His Spirit. Your only reputation should be a clean heart before God. Will you be remembered for your great love? We are commanded to love one another. Love does not sin. It can't.

Second, learn to love all you meet without expectations from them. Love because you want to love them. Give because you want to bless them. Bless them to truly let them feel blessed. Then let it go. If they love you back, then it feels like such a blessing to you, because you didn't demand it. It is received as a gift.

Set yourself free from the pain and torment of unfulfilled expectations from others. From this place, you are free to just enjoy being you with the freedom to love everyone you meet without reservation.

Lastly, know and trust that your sacrifice will be rewarded. You can not plant seeds of love all over your life garden and not receive a harvest much greater than what you have planted. It is a law.

***

Father, Thank you for sending Jesus to be our example of a life lived without the desire for a reputation before man, and for showing us what it looks like to love without conditions. Help us to follow You in this, and discover the great freedom and joy that is found there. In Jesus' name, Amen

Boundary 5: Fear Of Pride

Human pride will be humbled, and human arrogance will be brought down. Only the Lord will be exalted on that day of judgment. Isaiah 2:11 NLT

He makes them turn from doing wrong; he keeps them from pride. Job 33:17 NLT

You will notice that as we go through these boundaries, they will piggyback each other. A lot of our issues can stem from the same root system.

It has taken me many years to agree with God to write these books that He had asked me to. I had to learn these lessons you are reading about first and I had to fully overcome the need of a reputation, or the fear of what reputation I might get, before I could be willing to lay my life out for all to see, not worrying about the outcome. I needed to share the good, the bad and the ugly in hopes that by sharing my journey, it might help someone else to grow even faster than I did.

Next on the list, I had to overcome my fear of pride.

I had been told by friends that I didn't have pride. That I was very humble. But I feared pride. I feared that I might feel proud of the things God was doing in my life because it became quite extraordinary.

When the healings and such first started happening, I did feel a little puffed up. The God of all creation was now using ME to do His work and after fearing that I had been disqualified as I shared in Boundary 3, then learning that I wasn't disqualified and God didn't hate me--no--He desired with all his heart to use me, I felt like I was in a high place for awhile. I felt special, even though I was still dealing with low-self worth.

I really hope I can help you understand just how much I was in a quandary during this long season of my life. It truly felt like I was being recreated. I had to unlearn many ways of thinking, feeling and believing while learning new over time--having to undergo huge transformations in my entire life dynamic. God would be completely shifting who would be a part of my life journey and who would not. It felt like moving from one country to a new country and culture. I had to learn how to live all over again and all along the way, determine what was truth and what was not. Thankfully, God is a keeper of His promises; He truly gives wisdom to those who ask, He truly leads by His Spirit and will lead one into all truth, providing me with teachers all along the way who would both support me and edify me greatly.

***

I had watched Todd White do videos of his work on the streets. So, when I started going out on the streets in the beginning, I videoed what I did. I posted it on YouTube. I shared them on my Facebook page. I was SO excited about what God was really doing! It was real! And I had to tell the world! Then when I sat at home, I found myself feeling kinda special. Like, look at me! Look what God is willing to do in my life. It made me feel like I had value. It would be a journey of a couple of years to understand that I *was* in fact special, but I was special right along side every single other child of God. I was now finally discovering that I wasn't "less" than them, not greater than them, but was equal in the sight of The Lord. AND these amazing moves of God were supposed to be every Christian's normal experience. It simply required faith coupled with action.

I tell you the truth, anyone who believes in me will do the same works I have done, and even greater works, because I am going to be with the Father.
John 14:12 (NLT)

There it is again, <u>anyone</u> who believes will do the same works. Interestingly; I did think God gave gifts, but I initially thought He only did it to very special people. I had to unlearn bad teaching and renew my mind with the real truth of God's word before I would be able to fully understand and grasp the incredible power that God declared was available to ALL of us. We just had to believe. I had to overcome the boundaries of my mind. This wasn't just for the specially anointed. The mass majority of those we think are 'specially gifted' are simply people who have discovered who they are in Christ. They found the truth that we are all given these abilities through Christ Jesus as we believe in Him and walk it out by faith.

It wasn't until God taught me how secure I was in His love (and that truly was the biggest key for me, becoming secure in His love), that I was able to then look out, see those He wanted to love, and enjoy the journey. I no longer needed to think about myself. I was free from the need to be special (knowing we were all special) and able to be love to the one in front of me.

***

Continuing with the beginning of this chapter, I had a strong fear of not being humble and falling into pride. So, one day, I just deleted all my work. It was my way of humbling myself and making sure I was doing things from the right motives. I regret deleting them now because I had captured some really cool miracles that are now lost forever.

Next, the fear of pride kept me from writing my books. I would cry before God telling him I didn't want to share my journal of testimonies because I didn't want people to think I was boasting. I had to learn the difference between boasting and testifying. That my heart was to build up others in their faith. Had others not shared their testimonies, I would not be who I am today. Not even close. I needed to read thousands and thousands of testimonies. I had the hardest time accepting that God did these things today, and so it took literally thousands of testimonies to help me accept it as truth and not just one, or two or ten people claiming something spectacular. I don't beat myself up too badly about this as Jesus knew it would take that many for His apostles too. That's one of the many reasons they got a full three years of daily walking side by side with Him to see all that He was given by Father God to do, to in fact prove that He is who He says He is. They were saturated with Him, His teaching and who they are in Him. He sent them out to walk it out while He was still with them so He could answer questions and fill them with truth. We, today, are to carry the torch and be a living epistle for others to watch and learn from as we ourselves follow Christ.

Years had now passed and God was now setting the stage for me to begin teaching all that He had shown me and share the ways He had healed me. It was time to testify, not just to those close to me, but to the world.

I will not die; instead, I will live to tell what the Lord has done. Psalms 118:17 NLT

But Jesus said, "No, go home to your family, and tell them everything the Lord has done for you and how merciful he has been." Mark 5:19

My mouth will tell of your righteous acts, of your deeds of salvation all the day, for their number is past my knowledge. With the mighty deeds of the Lord God I will come; I will remind them of your righteousness, yours alone. O God, from my youth you have taught me, and I still proclaim your wondrous deeds. So even to old age and gray hairs, O God, do not forsake me, until I proclaim your might to another generation, your power to all those to come. Psalm 71:15-18 ESV

Sharing what God has done is not pride. It is testifying. It only becomes boasting when you are doing it to gain attention for yourself. Testifying is to put the light on Jesus Christ.

In the beginning, I needed others to see me. It was because I needed something from them. I had low self worth and needed to feel loved and valued. Because of this, God worked overtime taking nearly everything and everyone I loved too much away from me so that I would look to Him to depend on Him to fulfill all my earthly needs. That sounds harsh, and it was a very hard time to live through, but I needed Him to do it. It was the only way He could prove to me that He really would fill all voids I thought I needed others to fill.

He would in fact prove to me that He is enough. When I felt lonely, He'd have someone call me. If I was discouraged, He'd send people to encourage me. If I had questions, He'd send me teachers, and the list goes on. I finally felt safe. I finally trusted Him. Once you feel safe in God's love and can trust Him with every part of who you are, where you go, what you become and what you experience, you are free to stop looking at yourself worrying about your needs or about being rejected by those around you. There is an incredible peace, complete without worry when you know God has laid out your path and is orchestrating everything as you completely surrender yourself to Him.

I became free from the fear of pride when I took my eyes off of myself and began living my life for others, trusting myself to Him.

The fall in Eden caused us to put our eyes on ourselves and become self-centered and always thinking about our wants, needs, desires, fears, and the list goes on and on. The greatest freedom comes when we no longer concern ourselves with ourselves, but instead are concerned with trusting God with all outcomes, choosing to follow Him and living to serve others as greater than ourselves. Put others first. Sacrifice what you want for the betterment of another. Stop hanging onto things. Let it go. Let go of holding onto people. Trust God with them. It is absolutely liberating!

Take some time to meditate on what I've just shared. Are you walking in the freedom you want right now? Are you peaceful? Or, do you worry and stress out? Stress and worry are key indicators that you do not trust God to love you.

Lastly, I found complete freedom from pride when my heart settled in the knowing that all that I am is because of God. He is the potter, I am the clay. He chooses if I am made for noble purposes or ignoble purposes. Therefore, if someone sees something noteworthy in me and comments to tell me so, I can accept the kind words they offer with grace without feeling any pride at all. Because I know, I would not be what they see if it were not for the Father who created me that way. God alone receives all the glory.

***

Father, thank You that You give each person the boldness to testify. It is the Spirit of prophecy who bears testimony to Jesus. Let us be fearless in testifying of all that Jesus has done for us, through us and in us. In Jesus' name, Amen

Boundary 6: Be No Respecter Of Persons

But if you favor some people over others, you are committing a sin. You are guilty of breaking the law.
James 2:9 NLT

What is the law he is speaking of here? It is the law to love your neighbor as yourself. All your neighbors.

The more time I spent on the streets, in my workplace, on Facebook and church loving people with the gifts God has given me, I discovered something about myself; I was being selective.

God began to do new work in changing me. He began to challenge me about this issue of being selective. He would ask me, "Why did you pass that one by?" And I would give Him excuses that I *knew* He would not receive. "Well, that person is older Lord, probably set in their ways."; Or "That person is always grumpy and I'm sure they will reject my offer to bless them Lord."; Or "That guy is busy Lord, I'm sure he won't be thrilled if I interrupt his day." But God wasn't having it. He would tell me, "Have you ever met anyone who didn't need love?"

Have you ever met anyone who didn't need love?

OUCH! I felt shame and had to really look at myself to realize that in reality, I just felt fear--fear of rejection. But I also saw that I had an issue with being a respecter of persons. I saw some people as more "worthy" of a gift of God's love and grace than others.

I had to spend time with God just looking at people, letting Him show me His heart about each one. I literally would go sit in a park, go to the mall, sit up town on a bench, sit at church and many other places, and just look at the people, letting God teach me about His love for each and every one of them. He had no favorites. He loved each one equally. From the greatest to the smallest, they all have a heart that needs God. I had to learn to accept people's differences and find their individuality beautiful and special and not be against someone who doesn't eat as I eat, or dress as I dress.

We in our self nature judge harshly those who are not just like us as if we are God and the standard of perfection lies in others being like us. If they are not, we judge them as someone we must fix and conform to our image. But the reality is, we all need to conform to the image of Christ. We are **all** on a journey towards perfection and **all** deserve honor and love for who we are in this moment of our growth towards that end. As I spent more time watching people, God began to reveal their beauty. Each one was beautiful to me. Each person, unique and special.

I also began to see only their hearts, their humanness. I no longer saw their clothes, their nationality, color of skin, tattoos or piercings, the suit vs. the homeless man's tattered clothing. I did not see them as male or female, gay or straight, clean or addicted, good or evil, righteous or unrighteous. I just saw a human being who had a heart that needed Jesus' love and healing.

God taught me that many people wear masks. That what I might initially perceive at first sight is not what is really there, but things are buried behind a facade. He challenged me to deliver what He had placed in my care (the gifts and the gospel wrapped in pure unadulterated love) even to those I felt would absolutely reject it. He told me to trust Him.

This all changed me-------deeply.

It was like the blinders of the world had been taken off and I now could see through truth in love, that each soul needed to know they are loved, valued, have a purpose and that God sees them. That He desires to reveal that He knows them and wishes to save them from all that binds them unto eternal life.

There is no higher class or lower class with Him. God loves us all.

Let me share a story here that will help to bring this home. I had been out on the streets this day doing evangelism. I saw an older gent sitting on the front steps to an apartment building. I looked at him and thought in my mind; "He's older...he's probably set in his ways and not interested in anything I have to say." I had no idea that God would use this moment to radically transform me. Here is the story as I wrote it in "My Supernatural Life."

> As soon as I introduced myself and told him that I was out praying for people who needed healing, he said loudly, "I've been waiting two weeks for you!" I said, "Excuse me? What?" He explained, He didn't want healing, just to talk to an active faith-filled Christian.

"Not one of them pew sitters", he said. I was a bit shocked by his response.

We had a long and enjoyable conversation together and towards the end, I asked him if I could pray for his restless legs (which he had disclosed to me in our conversation). He wasn't concerned about getting healed, but allowed me to pray anyway. We took each others hands and I prayed a short prayer of healing and blessing. When I stopped praying, he began. As he was praying for God to send two angels to go out before me wherever I go, I felt power come FROM HIM into ME! I was like WHOOOOA!! I said, "You are a power-filled man of God!" I told him he still had work to do and that is why I felt God was preserving his life so well (he was elderly). We finished our talk (which was quite pleasant and edifying) and went our separate ways. I can't prove it one way or another-- but I wonder if he was an angel….

Do not forget to show hospitality to strangers, for by so doing some people have shown hospitality to angels without knowing it.
Heb.13:2 (NIV)
(end of excerpt)

Look at all that I would have missed out on had I allowed my judgement of him to win me over.

God would teach me as I continued to step out in faith to bless others that many many times, I would not be the only one to give away treasure. There are hidden treasures inside of all people. It is not just in sharing our faith that we need to be no respecter of persons, but in all aspects of life. Love sees only another heart that needs love. You can read God's thoughts in the story of the good Samaritan in Luke 10: 25-37.

It is something that we must become conscious of and put into practice. Are we withholding love? Why? What are your conditions for giving something good to someone else? Do you withhold a smile? Kindness? Good service? Why? To walk fully as a child of God, we are to withhold love from no one.

I heard something recently that gripped my heart. A man was talking to a woman about love. Did she really love greatly? She exclaimed, "Yes!" That she loved her children so much that she would die for her child if need be. And the man said, "But would you die for someone else's child? What about your enemy's child?"

***

Father, You hate wickedness in Your children. Withholding love when we have the ability to love is hatred. Help us to become willfully blind when it comes to the outward appearance of a man, but to only see a heart that needs to be loved. Help us to freely give what we are capable of, and to give without reservation, without any expectation of a return. How freeing and liberating it is to no longer judge if a man is worthy, but to live free to simply give to all whom we see. Transform our hearts to resemble Your heart Lord, and fill our hands that we may give it all away to bless another. In Jesus' name, Amen

Boundary 7: Fear Of Lack

Now you have every spiritual gift you need as you eagerly wait for the return of our Lord Jesus Christ.
1 Corinthians. 1:7

The fear of lack can be absolutely stifling. This fear had layers to it. I feared that I did not possess God's gifts, which are:
1. The word of wisdom,
2. Word of knowledge,
3. Faith,
4. Gifts of healing,
5. Working of miracles,
6. Prophecy,
7. Discerning of spirits,
8. Different kinds of tongues,
9. and Interpretation of tongues, (1 Corinthians 12:7-11)

Not only did I fear that I didn't have any of God's gifts, I felt I lacked in ability. I am introverted by nature. Those who meet me in person would never guess that. They think I am a very outgoing extroverted personality. And I am, around people I know. What most don't know, is that I find being in groups of people very taxing. I enjoy it for a little while, but then I really want to get away from everyone and get alone with God. I can spend hours and hours and hours alone in silence with God.

So, when I felt like God had called me to pray for people on the streets and everywhere I was, I was both excited and very stressed.

Because I am introverted, when I go out in public, I tend to mind my own business. I become tunnel visioned. The world just disappears while I get my shopping done. I get what I need and go home.

When I started to go out to do street ministry in 2009, I felt very stressed; very insecure because I lacked people skills.

God sent them out in two's for many very good reasons. One of those reasons is that you just feel more secure. I am fearless when I am out with another person, but 99.8% of the time I am on the streets alone. I don't have time to 'set up' outings. Living a Supernatural lifestyle means, you do it as you live out your everyday life. It isn't 'set apart' time, it's ALL the time.

On the days that I actually did set apart time for the sole purpose of ministering to strangers, I would literally sit in my truck for long periods of time trying to figure out how to introduce myself to them. I would drive to a location away from home, pull in somewhere, park, and then stress out. How do I start a conversation that would lead to me getting to pray for them? I cried a lot in my prayer time with God. I kept telling Him, "If this is truly my calling, shouldn't it be easier? Shouldn't I be fearless and super bold like so and so? Why is this so hard for me to do and yet I can't resist the call to go do it?" I felt like a lunatic being pulled in two directions.

God spoke to my heart even way back then and told me that I would be used someday to help others who also feel this same way. I would learn over the years of working through my boundaries, that those of us who feel we were only given one talent (and not the one we thought we needed), can actually do much if we are willing to fight to overcome where we feel we have lack.

My belief that I had lack was tormenting though. Some days, I would sit for over a half hour before I got the guts to even get out of my truck. Some days, I would get out, but never get the guts to speak to anyone. Looking like a whipped puppy, I would go home defeated and depressed that I couldn't do it. I just couldn't engage people. I didn't know how. The next time I'd go out, I would get up the guts to speak to one person and then that was all I could handle. I would go back to my truck and celebrate! I did it! I spoke to a stranger and didn't die! Whoo hoo!

The next form of lack for me was, I felt I didn't have the gifts. I had a lot of ideas in my head as to why I didn't have the gifts.
I was a woman. God's apostles were men and I thought for sure so were the 70 others he sent out. I explained more on that in Boundary 1, "Power of God not for today" and Boundary 2, "Hey God...I'm a woman!"

.
I thought I needed an impartation. In my mind, the gift had to be given. Because of Boundary 3, "Sins Disqualified Me", I wasn't sure God would let anyone give me the gifts I sought. And even if He did, my low self esteem said, it wasn't really for me. They were just being kind, but it didn't really happen. Listen you guys, I was a hot mess! That is why I am SO determined to help those I can. I guarantee you, If God could fix and use ME, He most surely can fix and use you!

***

If I do a good enough job writing this book, you will soon figure out that everything either flows or is stifled by what you believe. What do you believe as truth?

This is going to sound crazy, but the way I learned to overcome lack, is to walk in what you perceive to be your calling and the gifts you desire as if you already have it.

Walk in what you perceive is your calling and the gifts you desire as if you already have it.

This is called faith!

Because I had this tremendous zeal to see God move in power IN SPITE of my perceived limitations, I would gather myself up and go out and pretend that I had everything I needed and would picture myself being the person I wished I was. Then I would force myself to engage people. AND IT WORKED!

***

Let me share with you a parable to help you to see how you can grow in the gifts of God.

Once upon a time, there was a wealthy man who owned a great business. They shipped large very weighty boxes full of all sorts of things all over the world. The boxes were too heavy for any man to move without assistance.

This man had two sons. He wanted both to work for him in his company, so he gave the mandate, "Go out into the yard and move the boxes to the appropriate shipping yards for shipping."

75

The first son says to the father, "Give me a towmotor and I will be able to do the work you have given me to do." But the father didn't budge. He simply waited for the son to do what he requested of him. Days, months and even years went by as the son would repeat to the father, " I am willing to go do the work you have requested of me, but the task is impossible without a towmotor. It is simply impossible without it." And so nothing was ever finished. The work given to this son was never done.

The second son, upon receiving the mandate to go do the work in the shipping yard promptly went out and began to push hard on the boxes. He would look for ways to get the job done, but to no avail. Day after day, month after month, the young man pushed and pushed and pushed. Though he could not get the boxes to budge, he wanted to please his father and he just knew that if his father told him to do it, then there must be a way to do it. And so he persisted in trying.

One day, the father looked out into the yard to see his young son who by use of his strength, had become quite strong, saw that this son was obedient in all things, that even if something asked of him was impossible, he would simply do what his father asked of him to the best of his abilities. He was trustworthy and faithful.
So the father orders that the son be taken and shown where the towmotor is kept and teach him how to use it.

***

I was the second son (daughter). I knew in my heart that God had given me a mandate. I needed to figure out a way to get the job done even though I didn't feel I had the tools to do it.

According to the scripture I gave at the beginning of the chapter, we have been given every spiritual gift. So if we have already been given every gift, then it remains to be, that we need to 'believe' that we have it! Once we believe we have it, we need to open it. We open it by our obedient effort and use. (At least this has been my experience; I know of others who have been accelerated to instantly have the gift in full manifestation, but this was not the case for me. So I suppose I am speaking to those who are walking the same walk I have.)

What do you believe? Do you believe that God will use you to do miracles? If you truly believe, you will walk as if you can do miracles. Do you believe that you can speak words of wisdom or knowledge? If you truly believe--you will begin to engage people believing God will give you what to say.

You may say, but I don't believe I have that gift. Well then you do not believe the scripture which said, "*Now you have every spiritual gift you need as you eagerly wait for the return of our Lord Jesus Christ.*"
Yes, you will have times where it doesn't happen. The Olympic triathlete started off as an infant not even able to crawl. He had to grow in strength and ability. Then he crawled until he grew again in strength and ability. On and on he went until finally he was an Olympic athlete.

***

In the beginning, I was so full of fear. I was NOT good at small talk. I am still not good at it in most settings. I prefer to listen (well, unless we are talking about Jesus and who you are in Him). I struggled to engage people in conversation. And especially to start it talking about their need for healing or an encouraging word from God. ALL the boundaries you will read in this book were the layers I had to overcome. But on top of my lack of speaking skills, I had to overcome the "thought" that I lacked God's gifts to get the job done. I didn't know then what I am teaching you now. I thought I needed an instant full manifestation in order to show I had it. I had to adopt the concept of just trying, and letting God be God. In time, things got easier. I had to learn to trust Him to show up. I had to learn to be OK if I fumbled, fell, scraped my knees, and down right missed it from time to time (can't move the box). And even now, as mature adults, we can still trip, fall or scrape our knees. But we have learned to brush ourselves off and just keep going.

The only lack we possess is the lack we believe in our hearts.

Jesus said, we have been given every spiritual gift. He also said, anyone who believes in Him shall do the things He has done and greater.

What did He say to believe? In gifts? In anointing? In abilities? In callings? In ordinations? In titles or offices? None of the above. He only said, to believe in Him.

When I step out in faith for anything, I do not do so believing that "I" have an ability or gift. I believe that Jesus said, it is finished. He said that if I believed in Him, He would come and live in me. He said He gave His Spirit to me. And so, of myself, I am nothing. Just as the moon is dead having no light of its own and only gets its light from the sun. I too, only have the light of God in so much as I let Jesus in to shine His light through me. By myself I am weak, but In Christ--the greatest Apostle, Prophet, Evangelist, Pastor and Teacher-- can express Himself through me as I put my faith in Him.

When you learn about all my weaknesses, it just shows how amazing Jesus is! In my weaknesses, He can show Himself strong. I have learned to accept my weaknesses and overcome them by faith in Jesus, NOT faith in myself. I know that as I overcome myself, He can and will show Himself strong in me. It is amazing in that, as I put my faith in Him and step out in that faith, I grow in my abilities too. Anything we practice, we become better at.

Jesus, by His Spirit, reveals Himself differently through each of us. Some never see certain gifts manifest through themselves. But the seed, the potential for it is there. How do I know--Because Jesus who is all things lives in you!

The more opportunities you give Jesus to move by His Spirit through you, the more opportunities you will get to see just what gifts He will work through you. That is how I have experienced all the things that I have. I just keep opening doors of opportunity for Jesus to be Jesus through me.

In Him, there is no lack.

***

Jesus, Thank you that You live in all who believe in You. I pray for boldness for each one reading this, to walk by faith, not by sight. To have faith for what they hope for, and as they walk out this faith, will see evidence of those things not yet seen.

There is no lack in Jesus. The God of all creation lives within us. Let us walk out our lives in such a way that shows the world that we believe this to be true. In Jesus' name, Amen

Boundary 8: Rebellion

I will cleanse them of their sins against me and forgive all their sins of rebellion. Jeremiah. 33:8 NLT

Rebellion can be both good and bad. In the ways that it worked for the good were when I would rebel against untruth--when I rebelled against the teaching that the gifts stopped with the apostles--when I rebelled against the ideas that I could not do something simply because I was a woman. Actually, I rebelled against any idea that said I couldn't do something. If you told me I couldn't do something, It was like you just dared me to prove you wrong.

I would learn over my lifetime that I really had a deep rebellion against any idea that something should be impossible for me. My thoughts on the matter were, if you believe you can't, you are right. If you believe you can, you are right.

I rebelled against the idea that I had to have a college education in order to run my own business. I couldn't afford college and was an average student in high school. But when the time came, my husband and I drew up the blueprint to build my boarding and grooming kennel and we built it from scratch. One board and nail at a time we built it ourselves, together. I've been open for 21 years now and love my job. It is more than a business. It is a place for me to meet and interact with people and get opportunities to be who I am in Christ Jesus. Not only do I get to serve them by doing an excellent job caring for their dog, but I get to minister to their emotional, spiritual and physical needs by prayer and chatting. I love to get up and go out to the kennel to work every day.

However, I also had some bad rebellion locked up inside. One of the reasons I decided to start my own business was because I really struggled to come under authority. Most of the time, the rules put into place made no common sense to me. Just being raw and honest here, I felt most of my bosses were lacking in the ability to be a boss. I felt their ideas on how things should be run were wrong or unfair to those under them. Not that I wanted that job, no way, but I always saw the flaws in their logic. Not only that, but there was a part of me that really struggled with forced structure, rules or boundaries. I enjoyed being free to be creative, to try new things. I liked to experiment with life. I needed to explore, and pushing the boundaries of limitations gave me an adrenaline rush.

I'm pretty sure this is a gift as it is one of the main reasons I had such zeal to see God move in 'impossible ways'. I struggled to believe that anything should be truly impossible and needed to test it out for myself. So, discovering that we had power in the name of Jesus to make cancer tumors melt and disappear was right up my ally.

However my bad rebellion created other problems for me. God requires obedience. Instant obedience. Consistent obedience. Trustworthy obedience.

I noticed that the reason God wasn't trusting me to move and flow in some things I had asked for, was because I would tell Him that He could trust me with it, but He would tell me right back that he couldn't. As I discussed this further, He showed me that we must be faithful in the little things before He could give us the bigger things.

He was working on my character.

Let my yes be yes and my no, no. If I promised to do something, I needed to keep my word. Not just to Him, but to all people. When He would put something in my heart to do, everyday tasks, I was to be obedient in doing it and do it well. I'm talking about simple things of life. He would put it on my heart to clean the house, but I wanted to go ride my horse. He would want me to pay the bills, but I hated dealing with money, so I would always put it off until the bills were late. OH how I rebelled! My intentions were always good. I always intended to be obedient and do the right things. But my actions didn't match up. I was selfish and lazy. If it didn't suit me, I didn't do it. I'd get to it later. I procrastinated, or just flat didn't do it.

Over and over, year after year, I would continue to make promises to do better and then continue to fall short and fail. This caused frustration as I wanted God to open doors for me to do things for Him and the doors remained closed. This caused me to learn another valuable lesson. People won't change until they are TRULY sick and tired of being sick and tired. I had to come to the end of my selfish rebellious ways, learning that they only brought me misery and grief.

What always blew me away was, God kept loving me in spite of me--undeserved, unmerited love.
I would have days where I would sit and cry and ask Him, "What is wrong with you? Why do you still love me? Haven't I failed you enough yet for you to move on and give up on me?" His love would come and cover me like a warm blanket. He would send people that day to edify me and encourage me to press on. He never gave up on me. He put it in my spirit the truth that I would continue to cycle through this until I won the battle. What changed me was twofold: I hated the

repetitive cycle I was in, and I was so moved by Jesus' unwavering encouraging love for me.

I grew to **love** Him being over me (as my authoritarian).

I grew to **want** to serve Him (come completely under that authority).

I grew to a place where it hurt me to hurt His heart and I knew my rebellion in disobedience in all the many many little things of daily life, hurt His heart. He wanted to bless me. But in His love for me, waited until my character could carry it.

I began the journey of forcing myself to be obedient in all the little things. I had to force myself to overcome laziness in doing good or what is right.

God told me one day, "Your obedience to what your husband asks you to do is a direct representation of what your obedience to me is." OH SNAP! I was THE WORST at procrastinating doing anything my husband asked of me. In this part of my life, I was still feeling it was detestable for Him or others to *tell* me what I had to do. God told me, "How you treat your husband, who you feel is imperfect, is a reflection of how you are treating me in your heart." I tried to call Him a liar--but that didn't work. I knew God couldn't lie. I told Him, "It's easy to love you, you are perfect and you get me. It's not as easy to love him in all things because he isn't perfect and he doesn't get me or treat me like you do." He repeated, "I want you to respect your husband by being obedient to the things he asks of you. This will develop your heart in true love. When you can perfectly serve someone who is imperfect, you can then serve the One who is perfect with a right heart."

Of course I did not tell my husband this. But from that day forward, I made a commitment to do just that. If my husband asked me to do something, I did it. I did it right then.

God had also asked me to treat my husband as if he were God Himself, and not just my husband, but *all* people. I was to learn the art of becoming a servant, treating all people as if they were royalty. He wanted me to be a blessing to their lives. So, I began this work as well. It would take over a year for the fruit to become evident. But the principle of sowing and reaping began to mature and manifest.

My husband began to change before my eyes. He now had a wife that he could trust and rely on. He now had a wife who treated him like a king, seeking ways to make his life easier and pleasant (I still have off days, he will attest to that, but I was much more consistent). It now bore fruit in that he began to do the same to me.

This also transferred to everyone around me. The more seeds of love I planted into the lives of others, doing all that I knew how to be a blessing to their lives, treating them with honor, no matter who they were, began to bear fruit as well. People everywhere began to love me back and pour good things into my life.

God was pleased.

I had passed the test.

I had overcome the power of rebellion, and gained wisdom along the way. God is a good good Father.

Perspectives

Whatever you do, do it from the heart, as something done for the Lord and not for people, (CSB)

One last tidbit here to finish this chapter out--God taught me that much of why we suffer in this life is because of our perspectives.

I wasn't gifted with the Martha Stewart gene. Therefore, I don't get a lot of pleasure doing house work. I like a clean house--just don't like to have to be the one to clean it. There are thousands of other things much more fun.

I can remember one morning when I was struggling, rebelling against the very idea of getting the house cleaned up. I needed to because I was hosting a house meeting that night and wanted it clean for both the guests and the Lord. Everything in me wanted to procrastinate and put it off. That's when the perspective shift hit me--I'm not cleaning my house for myself. I'm not cleaning it just for the people, although they are surely a part of it. No, I wanted it beautiful and clean to create a habitation for the Lord. I want Him here!! I love, love, love His presence! I love to spend time with Him! And so, I wanted Him to see how much I valued Him by putting in the time and effort to get my house in order.

When He feels I have prepared a place for Him, He comes in greater weightiness and the people get what they need as a byproduct of His presence. All the time I am cleaning, I am thanking Him. Thankful that I have a house to clean. Thankful for what I know He will do when everyone comes that night. I turn on worship music and He and I occasionally dance together as I switch from cleaning one room to doing another. We enjoy one another in the process. I stay mindful of Him. As He puts people on my heart, I pray for them. We just hang out. When I am mindful of Him in these ways, it becomes joyful to do the work.

I have found that our minds are very powerful in how it can make us feel in any given situation. If we can change the perspective, we can find pleasure in doing what would have otherwise caused us grief. Rebellion changed into a time of enthusiasm, expectation and pleasure.

This is the Christian life. Abiding with God, with Jesus, with the Holy Spirit, changes everything for the better. I promise!

***

I pray that rebellion is crushed. That all who call on the name of Jesus learn the joy of obedience. Obedience creates a happy heart, and we feel no fear in approaching God or asking Him for things because our hearts are at peace before Him. Help us to grow in self-control, servant-hood and a heart that desires to live for God and others over ourselves. The fruit that is born from this is beyond our ability to understand or see until it matures. Let us be patient in doing good knowing there is a sure reward.
In Jesus' name, Amen

Boundary 9: Living For Myself
Developing the servants heart

Sitting down, Jesus called the Twelve and said, "Anyone who wants to be first must be the very last, and the servant of all." Mark 9:35 NIV

Humility isn't thinking less of yourself, but rather thinking of yourself less.

One of my great hopes in writing this book, is that you the reader will see that we can, at any time, change who we are. We can change how we think, what we believe, how we want to respond to life, how we treat others and so much more. We have the power to become who we want to become and do anything we put our heart into. You are not stuck being what you currently are. But, it will take effort to change. And some of the processes are painful.

The greatest among you will be your servant. Matt 23:11

This isn't about having a desire to be first. It's about the heart. God is looking for the right kind of heart. The reason He stated that the greatest among you is the one who is serving you, is because the servant is humble, meek, lowly, willing to suffer loss for another, willing to lay down his life, ie; lay down his own desires, his own dreams, his hopes or comfort to benefit someone else. The servant is willing to give the best to others and take the least for himself--or nothing at all if need be. It is a laid down life.

God knows that If every person everywhere lived in this way, no one would ever feel any need. We would all faithfully take care of one another. There would be no stealing, because we would all share everything we had. There would be no coveting others things for the same reason. No more my stuff (only) and your stuff (only). We would use our assets to benefit one another. It's an incredible place to be. No one would suffer from lack.

We have this relationship with our next door neighbor, Jimmy. We own various machinery on our farm and he owns various machinery on his. We have an understanding between us concerning certain machines, access to tools and such, and because of it, neither of us have to even ask the other before borrowing those things, just like family. We show mutual respect and take great care of each others things. I remember earlier this summer, Jimmy told my husband he was thinking of purchasing a skid steer and John's response was, "Why, when you can borrow mine any time you want?"

This is how it should be with all of us.

Another example of selfless living is sharing what you know. I wanted to be able to create my own covers for my books be- cause I like being creative, but didn't have a clue how to get started. I have a friend however, Mr. Michael Van Vlyman, who has written many books and creates all his own covers. I convinced him to let me come to his home and spend the day with him so he could show me how to get started. I'm a visual learner and need to see it and do it to get it. He showed me what programs to use, and how to make the programs do really amazing things.

The cover of this book is my first attempt after our lesson. Mike critiqued my attempts, offering suggestions until I settled on this one. He has been a great friend to me by sharing what he knew.

***

This chapter wouldn't need to be written if this was what I believed all along. So let's go back in time a little bit and see where my mind started.

I struggled with being truly selfless. It goes against the sin nature to serve others in sacrificial ways. Occasionally, I saw glimpses of the beautiful selfless heart in people around me and would think to myself, "They are such beautiful giving people, I wish I were like that." It seemed to come easy for them to want to make other people's lives comfortable and full. It seemed they did it without thought. That is where I differed. It took a conscious effort for me to think of putting others first. I just seemed to be naturally selfish and was competitive. Having two brothers and being born a girl in a man's world, I developed a very strong competitive nature that said, "I can and I will win and gain the prize--for me!"

I'm not sure when it started, but it seemed like my oldest brother and I had an unspoken war of, who will be the best at (fill in the blank). Everything in life was a competition to be better than someone else.

Competition isn't always bad. Having a competitive spirit can work to your advantage as it drives you to become your best. I just had to change my heart from being in competition against other people, to being in competition with myself. My goal had to change from being above others, to accelerating others, while advancing myself in growth to learn what love really looked like.

It is important for each of us to become all we were born to be. It just doesn't have to be at the expense of someone else.

It's interesting how getting close to Jesus will change you. My mind is traveling back to my youth, when my definition of love was more sensual. Love was confined to a feeling or a physical pleasure. As I spent more and more time alone with Jesus seeking truth about what love was, He began to do this work in me about becoming a servant. I wouldn't know for a few years after beginning this work, just how much it would change my heart and who I would become or how I would see other people and the world I lived in.

It started with simple things. God would put it on my heart to give up the best plate of dinner to someone in my family I liked least at that moment. Ever have a bad day with a family member? Of course you have. Well, because I cooked dinner, I knew which pieces of chicken were ju-u-ust right and which ones were a little burnt. My selfishness ran deeper than I thought. I can remember being angry and disgruntled when I put that best piece of chicken on the plate of the one I was angry with that day when I really wanted it for myself knowing how amazing it would taste. I ONLY did it out of obedience to God, and ONLY was obedient to God because I myself had wanted to grow and change. I wanted the change badly enough that I was willing to suffer a bit to see where this would go. The kick in the teeth was when I would give that best piece to the other person only to have them say, "It would have been better if…" THEY DIDN'T EVEN APPRECIATE IT! UGH! Boy, did God have work to do in me. I felt like it was a waste of my time to do good for others who didn't appreciate it. But in time, I would learn that love isn't about getting a return on your investment. Love just gives for the purpose of loving. It took time for my heart to really accept this new truth and not feel hurt or upset when my love was not received the way I thought it should be. I was still expecting a return on my investment.

The next thing God asked me to do was to become a listener.

I was a talker, and I would many times cut people off in order to be heard. My husband would tell me from time to time that he didn't like that I had that habit. It was rude, he said. But I just didn't see it at the time. I was too self absorbed. It wasn't until God connected me with a group of men who wanted to work together to do ministry that my desires to change and improve on myself really accelerated. One night, I was talking by phone with one of these gentlemen, Mr. Will Riddle. He was so beautifully delicate in how he would say things to help me see where I needed to improve. He began to teach me about having a pastor's heart. That all of us should develop a pastor's heart. He said, "Pastors are great listeners." That my homework was to grow into being a great listener. He said, "You will know when you have graduated at this when someone says to you, 'you are a great listener'." Well, I hate to say it, but it took around three years for me to hear that from a lady. Not that I hadn't been working on it all that time. I had been. But it takes time for something like this to become a recognizable stand-out trait about you. <u>There is a big difference between just keeping your mouth shut as you waited for an opportunity to speak, (which was what I was doing in the beginning) to *truly* listening.</u> People can tell the difference. Listening--forsaking saying what you'd like to say for the sake of someone else to be heard, is a sacrifice and it is love.

***

Next, I remember the Holy Spirit nudging me to offer to help people whenever a need was expressed. This was hard for me because not only was I dealing with being introverted, finding it more comfortable to keep to myself, I also felt inadequate in my abilities to help others. God desired to grow me past both.

First, I had to start listening more closely for opportunities to help to arise. One of the greatest tools to my growth was that at every request of God's Spirit for me to do this new homework, I would ask Him to please make me aware of missing the mark, or aware of the moment I was to initiate the new task. He was faithful.

I began hearing people state their needs. Then, I had to force myself out of my comfort zone (fearing rejection or fearing being inadequate) and offer to help. After a few times of being successful around people I knew, it then advanced to being watchful out in public for strangers. This was HUGE for me. Not only was there the fear of being rejected by strangers simply because we have all been taught to fear one another, but it caused me to face all my fears at once. Rejection, inadequacy, staying hidden (introverted), rejection, fear of the unknown, and did I mention rejection. But God had been teaching me that the only way to change and become something new was to overcome fear and get out of the old rut, which was my normal deeply dug in way of going.

I had to become comfortable with being uncomfortable. I had to become OK with what I perceived to be failure.

I would learn that what I thought was a failure, was not a failure at all, but growth. Sometimes you will need to 'fail' a thousand times before you 'succeed', not realizing, *the journey itself is success.*

Some of these changes God asked of me caused great stress in the process, but the stressful moments brought me into a journey of learning I could trust Him; that He was helping me to find Him; *to find what love really looked like,* and that as I continued to change in these ways, I would in time, find the freedom I had no current ability to even comprehend. I was following God by faith. My motivation to do it all was, I *had* to know what God's kind of love looked like.

As I began to reach out to strangers to offer assistance, I noticed something very special. Most were very grateful. Even if they said, "No, I'm fine." They would say, "Thank you for asking though," and they would smile at me. This filled me with joy!

I would find more and more as I learned to give away my best, be a good listener, and to be a help to those around me, that my reward was the *joy* I felt in being a blessing to someone else's life.

These tasks were just the beginning. The starting point to many more revelations of how I could find countless ways to lay down my life for the benefit of others.

***

God used my dog to teach me about lowliness in servant-hood with a right heart. I was in prayer before the Lord. I had no shoes or socks on so my feet were bare. While I was deep in prayer, my Border Collie comes and lays on the floor next to me as she often does. All of a sudden, I feel her begin to lick my feet. I usually stop her from licking at all because I don't particularly care for it. But the Lord impressed upon me to let her continue. I tried to remain focused on my time in prayer, but I couldn't shut out the fact that she was being very thorough in washing both of my feet for me. She would repeatedly go from one to the other to make sure she got them both, top to bottom and every toe. Then it hit me--God was using her to wash my feet!

He was revealing a moment of what it is like to serve someone completely, contentedly from a loving heart. He then caused me to focus my attention on the fact that she was using her tongue to wash my feet. Would "I" be as lowly as she? Now God isn't asking us to use our tongue to wash others' feet. Not at all. The point is; She had no other resources to bless me with, so she used all that she had. Out of her poverty of not having human hands, she did with what she had. And even so, she was completely content with her task. She never once thought to herself; "This is gross, I can't believe I am doing this." She found a way to show her love and servant-hood to me in that moment with who she was and what she had available to her.

The lesson He brought to light is: Will you humble yourself and use what you have to bless another. Will you become lowly to reveal love? How lowly? What thoughts will be going through your mind as you do so? Will it bring you pleasure to just be a blessing to another?

No matter your poverty in the moment (poverty meaning your assets, physical ability, disability or position in life), you can find a way to serve another. We are told to be humble and lowly in this way, not seeing ourselves as lower; nor higher than anyone else. Each one should serve the other as though they were higher and yet your brother.

Know also, we are all equal in the sight of God. Jesus said, *"But do not be called Rabbi (Teacher); for One is your Teacher, and you are all [equally] brothers. Do not call anyone on earth [who guides you spiritually] your father; for One is your Father, He who is in heaven. Do not let yourselves be called leaders or teachers; for One is your leader (Teacher), the Christ. But the greatest among you will be your servant. (Matt 23: 8-11)*

It's food for thought--is my dog who has no inheritance in the kingdom, demonstrating servant-hood better than we are?

***

So how can you tell when you are in self? Here are some clues to help you on your journey.

*Anytime you place your wants above the wants of others.
*Anytime you place your needs above others.
*Anytime you place your desires above others.
*Whenever you feel something isn't fair, you are in self. You need to lay it down.
*When you get angry (like when the guy pulls out in front of you and makes you need to slow down to let him in), ninety nine percent of the time anger is because you are not getting your way. Check your heart. Oh! The gift of letting go of

anger--camp out here as long as it takes to forgive yourself and others. Just let it go. It is worth it.

*Anytime you feel the need to be in control of someone else.

*If you hold bitterness, you are in self.

*If you covet, want what someone else has for yourself.

* If you feel pain if something or someone is taken away from you. You are in self.

*Holding Resentment

*Envy

*Needing to dominate

*In your rush....you disregard others.

*Anytime you do anything for yourself at the expense of another

*Unforgiveness

This list could go on and on. But these are some points that you can look at and spend as much time as you need to meditate on and implement change in your life to overcome it.

In order to change, you must find an action you can implement in each area to develop a new heart. Your eyes will open and you will begin to see differently. You will be set apart from the world,--In it, but not of it.

This is ongoing. I can't tell you that I have mastered overcoming self. But I can tell you that as I have grown in awareness coupled with putting forth the works to change, I am seeing life from new eyes and experiencing it from what I call a higher place. Growing from glory to glory.

I've learned the lesson of planting and reaping. In the beginning of each of these transitions, you will at first suffer loss.

As you empty your pockets of all the seeds you have to give, they go into the ground and you can no longer see them. They stay hidden for what seems like a very long time. It is out of your hands (it hurts to suffer loss--be willing to hurt). Just as the farmer's seeds planted in good ground will come up on it's own, grow as a seedling, develop a stalk and then at the right time, produce a harvest much greater than what was planted, so too, these seeds of change will in time produce a harvest of peace, joy, tranquility, happiness and freedom. You will learn and understand what love really is. You will become a vessel of true love.

I learned how to separate myself from the world's ways. No longer needing to be above others to be successful. Instead, discovering the great joy that can only be found with a true servant's heart.

When you expect nothing from others, they cannot hurt you. You are free to serve them in love purely as a gift. One of my greatest joys, is in accelerating others.

Plant love, friend. Then wait……………….

Jesus is the greatest servant of all. Laying down His life for His own creation who despised Him unto crucifixion. Then He rose from the dead, defeating death and sin so that those very people could be brought to the Father as family for eternity. Let us aspire to love both our friends and our enemies as Jesus did.

***

Father, it is my heart that You give peace to my brother or sister reading this. Encourage them all along the way just as You did for me. Give them strength to do things in a new way. If we keep doing what we have always done, we will keep getting what we've always gotten. It's not easy to change. There is fear of loss, fear of the unknown. But Lord, You did not give us a spirit of fear or timidity, but of power, love and self-discipline. Help them to find the joy You've given me in accelerating and advancing others. It is in growing others that we ourselves find that we too have grown and are accelerated. Bless this reader now Lord, In Jesus' name, Amen

Boundary 10: Can't Hear God

My sheep listen to my voice; I know them, and they follow me. John 10:27

For those who are led by the Spirit of God are the children of God. Romans 8:14

So I say, let the Holy Spirit guide your lives. Then you won't be doing what your sinful nature craves. Galatians 5:16 (All NIV)

The truth is, we can all hear God. We just have to listen. We need to trust.

Part of my testimony is that I complained to God that I couldn't hear Him. But the truth was, I didn't *trust* what I was hearing was Him. In the last decade, I have greatly developed hearing God for my life. I first had to develop practicing His presence. Meaning, I had to develop my thoughts to always, always, always be aware that God was with me. He is omnipresent. Always present. Never not present. He is everywhere I am at all times no matter what I am doing.

From this perspective, the next thing I had to overcome was the religious part of me that had been taught that praying to God meant going somewhere and getting on my knees, folding my hands together and closing my eyes while I spoke in King James type talk to some being way up in the sky somewhere hoping He could hear me. It went something like this, "Dear heavenly Father, most holy God, hear me O Lord, Jesus. I prayeth Jesus that you forgiveth me Jesus, touch me and bless me Jesus. Oh Jesus you art faithful Jesus, thou art the one who saves me Jesus. ---OK, you get the picture. Well one day I heard Jesus laughing at me. Not being mean, but like a big brother looking at this little sister who just didn't get it yet. He stopped me mid-prayer one day and said, "Listen to yourself. What do you think your friends would do if you talked to them like that?" He asked me to picture myself standing right in front of my husband and He went on with, "Oh John, I pray you heareth me John. My beloved husband, John. Oh how I loveth you John. I need breadth from the store, John. Oh John could you blesseth me by going to the store, John? Oh John, I need help my beloved John, could you help me, John?"

My eyes got so wide! I was like--OH MY GOODNESS! I told Him, "I thought you liked that?" But yeah, to talk like that to anyone else just sounded stupid. I didn't realize just how many times I said His name in a sentence. It was like I wanted to make sure He knew I was talking to Him and only Him. But He wanted me to see how I would respond if someone did that to me. I said, "I'd just tune them out. I'd be annoyed."

Over time we would have many talks about how I was to engage Him. God is multifaceted. He is King, Father, Husband and Friend (as a short list). And in this season He would teach me to come to Him in different ways at different times for different purposes. At this time, He was looking for me to experience Him more as a friend. He wanted me to learn the art of praying without ceasing.

What did praying without ceasing look like? I surely did not have the time to sit on my knees all day. He would teach me to think of Him as my good friend, a life partner who wanted to go through life with me, who wanted to be a part of everything I was doing everyday, and that He got joy in being with me. He reminded me that the Holy Spirit was sent to be my teacher. I should start asking questions.

So I did.

This was when life became so much more amazing! I began talking all day everyday about everything. We would sit outside together and talk about the birds, trees, bushes, grass, water, wind, you name it. I did most of the talking. He mostly spoke by opening my eyes to truths.

God "speaks" differently than we do. He is not limited by speech. I would learn that He would speak to me in countless new ways.
He would speak by implanting thoughts;
Giving impressions;
Give heart unctions/gut feelings;
In dreams, visions and mind pictures;
Through my emotions (at times he would have me feel the emotions of the one I was speaking to so I knew how they felt and therefore, knew how to minister to them);
He drops in ideas;
Reveals secrets--His, and sometimes of people near me;
Knowings (you just know stuff);
Leads by strong desire to do things;
Single word of knowledge;
Drops names in my heart that He wants me to call or pray for;
Invasive thoughts; (give directions by having a thought pop in while I am in thought about something else);
Changes in atmosphere;
Tingling in or on parts of my body that we understand together what it's for;
Feeling pain where someone else has pain;

Smelling fragrances;
Awareness--He will make me aware of things;
Road signs, TV, Radio hosts, songs, license plates, etc;
Discernment, when He reveals what spirits are active in people or places;
And of course, His Word.
I'll stop there, you get the idea now. It really is limitless the ways God can speak and reveal what He wants you to know.

Being led by the Spirit takes faith--just being open for God to be God without us getting in the way. It takes overcoming fear. Religion will limit you by causing fear to do anything for fear of being outside of God. But that's where relationship comes in. God knew how terrified I was of doing anything that was not of Him. I prayed daily for Him to keep me close and never let me be deceived. Accuracy in hearing Him would be proven by the fruit it bore. Every time God spoke in a new way and I trusted by stepping out in faith, He would prove it was Him by the fruit it bore. People got healed and they got delivered and grew closer to Him. The more this happened, the more I trusted and opened myself for more. "How big are You?" I'd ask. "I want to experience all of You." I'd say.

When I first started learning all of this, developing a life of being led by the Spirit, I would at times get upset that it seemed God was not speaking, or was not giving me full answers. My friend Joel told me to start asking yes or no questions. You will feel it in your heart if it is a yes or a no. This helps your heart to learn to trust you can in fact hear. He went on to say: "If you don't feel a check in your spirit that is a distinct no, then follow it as a yes and see where it goes."

I started to ask God to give me ideas when I would be out working my horses or working with dogs during work. He would at times give me an outright answer to my problem by making a suggestion. Or He would answer my question with a question. He wanted me to think and process the situation and show myself I already knew the answer, I just needed to accept it and act on what I knew inside was right.

Because I struggled to trust that the still small voice inside was actually God, I made a deal with Him one day. I told Him that from that day forward, the first thought to come to me after I asked Him a question, I would attribute that to Him. I would follow that first thought with faith believing it was Him. If I was wrong, then I trusted He would make things right as I tried to follow Him in this way. I would quickly learn the truth of the scripture that read, *"The mind-set of the flesh is hostile to God because it does not submit to God's law. Indeed, it is unable to do so." CSB*

The carnal mind is enmity against the Spirit of God. I found this to be a fascinating way to kind of check which voice I was hearing. The Spirit of God is all about restoration, healing, deliverance, doing good, being kind, being faithful, being gentle, bringing joy, peace and love. But the carnal mind will come against walking out things of this nature. So, when that first thought came in and wanted me to do something that fell in line with God's Spirit, but then the very next thought ALWAYS came against that, I knew the first thought was of God and the second was of my own sin nature.

Example: "God, do you want me to reach out and pray for that person over there?"

A. I begin to feel compassion for the person, sadness that they have a need for healing. I feel no check in my spirit against it (this is all part in how God speaks).
B. So, as I ponder what I am feeling, my carnal mind chimes in and says, "They will not receive you. They will probably be annoyed at being bothered. They are busy shopping. It probably won't work anyway."
C. This question shouldn't have needed asking in the first place as you will find it in God's word that we are to love one another. So of course the answer was yes without Him needing to say anything.

Has this ever happened to you? You KNOW in your heart that it is good for you to love another by praying believing for God to touch them, you know that He desires to reveal Himself to them in these special and unique ways, but your carnal mind will instantly come against your stepping out and doing good. This is how I know that I am to follow the first thought or inclination I get after asking the question.

The following is an example of an interjected thought. I have two stories I will put here. Both had to do with my animals.

First one: It was winter, snow covered and cold. I was sitting on the couch watching TV with my husband when all of a sudden I think, "the chickens are thirsty, they have pooped in their water pan and won't drink it." At the same time I have this thought, I "see" them in my mind's eye like you would do if I were to say, "kitten". You instantly can picture a kitten in your mind. This is the same here. I saw the chickens walking around the waterer wishing for a drink. I kind of blew it off as me just being a worry-wart about the care of my animals. It could wait until I went out later that night at regular chore time. As I sat there a bit longer, the thought pops in again, "The chickens are thirsty, they have pooped in their water pan and won't drink it." The thought sounds like my own voice, but the interesting factor was, I was busy thinking about something else when it would "interrupt." This time, I told God, "I think this is you, so I'm going to follow it." I got up, got my coat and boots on and went out to the chickens. They had in fact soiled their pan badly. I dumped it, cleaned it, and put in fresh water. I no more than got it sat down and every chicken in the coop rushed over and drank deep!

The verse: *"What is the price of two sparrows--one copper coin? But not a single sparrow can fall to the ground without your Father knowing it." Matthew 10:29 NLT*

God cares about every life and He knew they were important to me too. So, He told me their needs. Not only did He demonstrate His love for the little things, but this also gave me a new way to trust hearing Him.

Second one: To solidify that I could trust these intrusive thoughts were of Him, He did it again. It was again a very cold winter day. I had a male rottweiler that lived outside. On really cold days I would take him indoors at night so he was nice and warm. On this particular day, it had been really nice out. But as the sun went down, it got cold FAST! Really cold. But I was unaware of it because I was sitting in my nice warm house watching TV with my husband again. I'm not a big TV person, but when my husband gets home from work, that is how he relaxes and I always sit with him for a few hours. Once again, as I am engrossed in what is going on in the house, a thought comes in. "Jake's cold." It catches my attention, but once again, I kind of blew it off at first because I was in the middle of the show. Again the thought comes in, "Jake's cold." I tell God, "I think this is you again. I'll go out now." I bundle up and go out. BRRR! I get to his pen and he is standing at the gate so happy to see me as he full-body shivered with the cold. I let him out and he joyously bounces all the way to the warmth of the indoors. Isn't God good!!!

I want to share another example of hearing God for you here. This is on how to be led by Him via Mind Pictures.
I am going to use an excerpt from my book, "My Supernatural Life", as I go into great detail there on various ways I hear God with personal testimonies. Here it is:

God wishes to be active in every aspect of our lives. Not just ministry. He is interested in you and just hanging out with you doing what you like to do.
So, one day I was gathering up tools and supplies to do a little construction project in my dog kennel. It is winter and I was losing too much heat through the dog doors.

My intent was to make the openings smaller and to construct plugs made with wood and 2" styrofoam to insulate it from the wind and heat loss. As I was gathering up the saws I would need, I felt led to grab a jigsaw. I had no apparent need for the jigsaw, but felt led to grab it anyway. So in obedience to that thought, I did.
I also needed a Miter saw and a Circular saw.
I couldn't find the Circular saw so I went without it for the time being.
My relationship with God is such that I talk to Him all the time as if He is standing right next to me every minute of every hour of every day. So, I'm chatting with Him about what wood I need.
I go to the utility barn and I start finding all the 2X4's I need. I was SO happy because in my treasure hunt I was able to find just enough wood to do my project without having to go shopping for it. It was below 0 out with wind chills in the -30 range and roads were drifted badly everywhere.
I measured and cut all my boards and felt accomplished. I started to put them in place when I got to the last few boards and made a grave discovery. I had cut one board 3" too short! I was reading the tape measure upside down and instead of cutting 29.5" I cut it 26.5" UGG! I had JUST the right amount of wood! So, I went back out in the cold and was thinking to myself, I wonder where else to look, when a picture popped into my mind. I saw myself walk

into my horse barn and that there was a board just inside the door on the left.

I started to dismiss it because I am in there every day and I didn't remember any lumber left in there. But in obedience to that picture that popped into my head, I decided to see if it was God. If so, this was a new way for us to talk. (I actually talked to God as I walked to the barn stating, I am just going to trust this picture is from You.) You guessed it, I walked into the barn and hidden behind some binder twine was a 2X4 that was perfect for my needs. YES! Thank you, Jesus!

So, I go back to work and as I am screwing the boards in place, I see I am not going to have enough screws to finish the job. So this thought pops into my head to go take one screw out of each of the boards I had already put into place. I do so and had exactly enough screws to finish installation. Many people would never give God credit for that thought. They would just think they were smart and figured it out on their own. But I know that all good things come from God and therefore I honor Him with the praise and glory due Him for even the smallest things. It is in the small things like this that God will do the great things in other areas because He knows we attribute these thoughts to Him and are instantly obedient to them. We are developing trust and relationship.

At this point, I took a little break and told God, I really need that red circular saw! At that moment a new picture popped into my head. I saw that it was in the back of my husbands old van in the front yard. So, in faith, I went out to the van. it was covered deep in snow and I had a really hard time getting a door to open so I could get in. But once in, I not only found the red circular saw, but I found more screws the length I needed and the bible I had been looking for (I have many translations and was looking for this one earlier)!

Finally, I needed to cut the foam and had been pondering the best way to do this when God reminded me of the jigsaw he impressed on me to bring out. It worked perfectly!

This was so much fun working side by side with my Father. He works in my life like this all the time! It is all relationship. By taking the time to learn to hear His voice in all these different ways, It has made my life an adventure. It always requires faith. God is moved by our faith.

This next mind picture story I will never forget! This is where learning to trust God in these things gets exciting and fun!

One day I was taking a new lady out to teach her how to minister on the streets. I took her into a WalMart store and I asked God for a picture of who He wanted us to minister to. I instantly got a very clouded picture, No details, all I saw in my minds eye was a woman about my height with a toddler in the front seated section of her cart. so, I told this to the lady with me and off we went looking.

It was amazing just how many mothers with toddlers there were in the store. They were EVERYWHERE! So, this lady friend starts pointing out women and toddlers and I would say, they're not it. She asked me how I knew. I said, I don't know, I just know I will know when I see them.

After awhile, I saw this toddler in a cart and I KNEW it was the right baby. but the mother was wrong. I began to walk away when who I thought was the mother walked away and another woman began pushing the cart. It was her! I never saw her clearly in my mind picture, but somehow I knew.

So, I stopped her and said, "Ma'am, you might think this is odd, but God hand picked you to receive a blessing today. I've come to pray for you. Is there something you need prayer for today?"

She looked at me dumbfounded and said, "What?" I repeated myself to her and then started to prophesy over her. This was in itself a HUGE act of faith for me because I was still learning to trust that if I opened my mouth, that

God would just show up. Why? because He loves THEM and wants them blessed and to know Him. It has nothing to do with me. Far from it!

So, I started to tell her that I knew she had been praying and praying and praying for some things and God wanted her to know He heard her prayers and was going to answer them.

She looked at me with this look that scared me! I thought she was mad at me. But then I saw the tears come.

She said, "Who are you?" I told her my name. She said, "You don't get it! I just got released from rehab. I am a heroin junky (she pulled up her sleeves and showed me all the needle tracks.) and they want to take away my little girl. My family is a wreck. I have been praying like 20 times a day to some God out there. I don't know His name or anything about religions, I just hoped there was something bigger than me out there that could help me and here you are saying this!!"

I smiled at her and said, "Yes, God showed you to me just now in the store in a vision and he sent me to tell you his name is Jesus and he loves you." (she made me repeat that as well, she just couldn't believe what she was hearing!) I then went on to share the gospel with her. I told her what Jesus did for her and what he wanted to do for her now. I prayed for her deliverance and for all traces of her past to be removed. That Jesus loved her and sought her out today to make himself known to her.

She left there changed on so many levels that I am sure I will not know the depth of it until I get home and God shows me.

I would have never experienced this had I not trusted that first cloudy, unclear vision and just stepped out in faith and obedience that God was going to do something if I did something first. Trust!

(end of excerpt)

***

Hearing God requires faith. It requires relationship and trust. In the beginning, I was so fearful of being wrong that it would many times hinder me and keep me from experiencing God's best. What made the difference for me was, I had an incredible hunger to know just how interactive God wanted to be with us, His children, AND I had equal hunger to reveal Him to the world as the true LIVING God. He is active in our lives and interested in communicating with us.

The sons of God are led by the Spirit of God. (Romans 8:14)

I don't know how people get through life without Him. It is by learning to trust that I heard Him and by always being obedient to the leading of His Spirit in all these fabulous ways, that I was able to grow in all the areas you are reading in this book and so much more.

The common thread that must be implemented is faith. In every form of communication, you have to first step out in faith believing, trusting. You have to take a risk. Risk being wrong. You will be amazed as you grow and develop your relationship with the Holy Spirit in this way, how amazingly you will be rewarded as He reveals all He is willing to do with you, through you and for you. Talk to Him.

***

Tips to begin:

1: Set aside time to be alone with Him as often as you are able. I spend time in set-aside prayer every morning before I rise and every night before I fall asleep.
2: Practice His presence. Be aware of Him with you everywhere you are all day long.
3: Invite Him into everything you do. Ask Him questions. What would you do, Lord? Then follow His leading by faith.
4: Talk to Him all day about everything like you would your best friend.

5: Step past the thoughts of your carnal mind. Be bold in doing good and what will bless others.
6: Develop your relationship with God believing He wants to speak to you.
7: Have faith. Trust He wants you to hear Him more than you want Him to speak.
8: Don't limit how He can 'speak'.

***

Father, thank you for being so willing to speak and lead us by Your Spirit. I ask you to create hunger in my brother/sister to hear Your voice in everything they do. Develop them in the subtle ways You speak. Confirm it for them so they can learn, just as You taught me, that what they are hearing is in fact You. Bless them on their journey in trusting You, In Jesus' name, Amen.

Boundary 11: Trusting God's Word To Be True
No matter what I see

Now faith is the substance of things hoped for, the evidence of things not seen. Hebrews 11:1

Another struggle I faced was what to do when what I *thought* should happen didn't happen.

As I began to stretch myself to believe that God would actually heal people instantly before my eyes, I had to deal with the evidence of what I saw. Remember, I had been taught that this all ended over 2000 years ago and now I was trying to rediscover the bible for myself through a new lens. Though I had seen much evidence through others and had experienced my own instant miracle when my genetically short leg grew out, I still had to learn to trust that God loved me this way (to do His works through me) and that I could trust what His word said;

"I tell you the truth, anyone who believes in me will do the same works I have done, and even greater works, because I am going to be with the Father. John 14:12 NLT

Jesus just said, "I tell you the truth" and God can't lie, right? Then He said, "anyone." That should mean me! That should mean you! God can't lie, right? He went on to say, "Will do the same works I have done." He was healing the sick, casting out devils, raising the dead, opening blind eyes and ears, knew people's thoughts and hearts, multiplied food, changed matter (water into wine) and imparted gifts to men.

While I do not believe that every Christian will do <u>all</u> these things, I do believe that as a *body* of believers, we can each walk in what we have faith for to reveal Christ. We all have our own gifts, talents, abilities, faith and testimonies that when used, will cause others to believe as well.

Let's look at more scripture to clarify.

7 Now to each one the manifestation of the Spirit is given for the common good. 8 To one there is given through the Spirit a message of wisdom, to another a message of knowledge by means of the same Spirit, 9 to another faith by the same Spirit, to another gifts of healing by that one Spirit, 10 to another miraculous powers, to another prophecy, to another distinguishing between spirits, to another speaking in different kinds of tongues,[a] and to still another the interpretation of tongues.[b]11 All these are the work of one and the same Spirit, and he distributes them to each one, just as he determines.

12 Just as a body, though one, has many parts, but all its many parts form one body, so it is with Christ. 13 For we were all baptized by[c] one Spirit so as to form one body—whether Jews or Gentiles, slave or

free—and we were all given the one Spirit to drink.
14 Even so the body is not made up of one part but
of many. 1 Corinthians 12:7-14 (NIV)

----

27 Now you are the body of Christ, and each one of
you is a part of it.28 And God has placed in the
church first of all apostles, second prophets, third
teachers, then miracles, then gifts of healing, of
helping, of guidance, and of different kinds of
tongues. 29 Are all apostles? Are all prophets? Are
all teachers? Do all work miracles? 30 Do all have
gifts of healing? Do all speak in tongues? Do all
interpret? 1 Corinthians 12: 27-30

We all have a part to play. I just happen to be of the mindset
that we shouldn't limit ourselves to just one thing. I
encourage you to be open to all that God may want you to
experience in Him.
Then there were more scriptures that I had to grow to
understand.

He said to them, "Go into all the world and preach
the gospel to all creation. Whoever believes and is
baptized will be saved, but whoever does not believe
will be condemned. And these signs will accompany
those who believe: In my name they will drive out
demons; they will speak in new tongues; they will
pick up snakes with their hands; and when they

drink deadly poison, it will not hurt them at all;

they will place their hands on sick people, and they

will get well." Mark 16:15-18 NIV

There, He said it again, "Whoever". Whoever is not gender specific. It means literally, whoever. Not only was Jesus setting me free from the chains the church had put on me because I was born a woman (limiting the way I could minister within the church walls), but it also did other things. Jesus spoke to my heart one day and said, "Look around you." When He said that, I saw the entire world. I knew that I was free to go into all the world and practice what I believed was placed in my heart to do.

I felt Jesus speaking to my heart saying, "No one can limit you but yourself. Go!"

I can remember feeling so blessed and free that I would be able to express myself and experiment with the gifts of God on anyone I met that day. And yes, it felt like experimenting. Each new person I prayed for was an experiment. What did I have faith for? What did they have faith for? Was the bible true? What would happen if I put my hands on them and prayed? What if I didn't touch them at all? What if I prayed out loud vs praying inside moving things with the intentions of my heart? What if I prayed in a text message or over the phone?

Then there were the other questions that came as a result of praying: Why did some feel something and get healed while others felt nothing and got healed? And the opposite was true: Why did some feel great power come on them yet no healing? Why was it that I would pray for one person with carpal tunnel and they got instantly healed and then the next person I prayed for with the same issue did not get healed? I know I keep reminding you of my low self esteem, but it's important here. When things didn't happen for people, I took it very personal. I had to dig deep and try to understand why the healing wasn't taking place. Was it me? Was it God? Were my sins really forgiven? Were their sins forgiven? Did I need more faith? Did they?

When someone didn't get healed, it really shut me down. It was incredible just how often God would send encouragement to me to keep going when I would get confused or discouraged. Him doing that over and over again was yet another tool He used to help me see that He was not the angry wrathful God I once thought He was, but that He was in fact my greatest encouragement and cheerleader.

I can't give you answers to some of the questions I had up there. No one really knows why some get healed while others don't. We are not God and do not know all that He knows about a person or their situations. I used to let what I saw with my eyes really get to me. For the longest time, I just felt it was my fault, and at times I'm sure it was. But what keeps me going is this; I am on a journey to love people with all that I have. I am growing in truth and in faith. The word of God is truth no matter what I see with my eyes. If someone does not get healed, the truth still stands that Jesus said, "Anyone who has faith in Me shall do what I have done and greater things." I believe that! Period!

My desire is to see everyone I pray for get healed, set free and delivered. My heart is to love them, and I have just enough fight in me that says, I will keep trying and growing until every impossible thing becomes possible. Love never fails.

If I am praying for a stranger on the streets and don't get to see a healing, the question is, did I love them? Love heals many things. That person might not get the physical healing I sought that day, but their spirit felt loved. It may be their spirit that needed healing on that day all along. I share a testimony of this kind in the Last Boundary/Chapter of this book.

There are many accounts when I would pray and not see an instant healing only to have the person find me days or weeks later to tell me that the healing happened the next day or a couple days later. Like the day I prayed for my Farrier who wore a knee brace. He told me he had had a bad knee for years and was on very strong medication both morning and night for the pain. I prayed for him and asked him to check it for healing. Nothing changed. I prayed three times for the knee, but no improvement. He left my farm and life went on. I remember feeling heartbroken that I wasn't walking in good enough faith to get him healed. A couple months later, we were both at a tack swap meet, he sees me and yells out, "Hey!" and points at his knee. He no longer had a brace on. He walks over and tells me, the next day after I had prayed for him he was pain free and hadn't needed any pain meds sense. The knee was like new. I was blown away! Here I had thought it was a failure and God brings the news to me that it in fact worked!

God was teaching me, never trust your eyes. Trust the word of God, be bold in loving people, believing God to love them more than you do. Be fearless in praying for someone to get healed. It's so easy. It doesn't have to be long or elaborate. Just pray what is on your heart to say. It can be as simple as, "I pray God blesses you and heals you, In Jesus name."Or just "Be healed, In Jesus name." Then ask them to check it. You may be surprised! Be led by God in love. Love never fails.

***

Father, Give us the faith to trust Your word to be true no matter what we see with our eyes. Help us to always pray believing by faith in Jesus Christ that what You have entrusted to us to do will be accomplished. You will in fact confirm Your word with signs following. May the Lord Jesus be glorified in all things, in Jesus' name, Amen

Boundary 12: The Heart

Carefully guard your thoughts because they are the source of true life.
Proverbs 4:23 CEV
Be careful how you think; your life is shaped by your thoughts.
Proverbs 4:23 GNT
But the Holy Spirit produces this kind of fruit in our lives: love, joy, peace, patience, kindness, goodness, faithfulness, gentleness, and self-control. There is no law against these things. Galatians 5:22-23 NIV

What I am about to share with you now, changed my life astronomically and is still unfolding in it's vastness. A little history to set the stage. I know a man who has a very close relationship with God. He spends countless hours in seclusion praying and worshiping him. One day he said to me very quietly, "I can hear people's thoughts." He said it just started one day. He shared with me how painful it was because his friends would be standing in front of him saying one thing with their words, but he could hear their true thoughts about him and it really hurt.

I am not here to argue with you whether God allows this or not. I know Jesus knew people's thoughts, and He lives inside of us. God can allow anything He wants, just as He did for Jesus.

Whether it's true or not in his case, is irrelevant. But the thought of it being true did something to me. I went home and in my own quiet time with God, began to judge my own heart. I began to think to myself: "What would life be like if *everyone* could hear my thoughts?" I made a decision that day, that I would live my life as if everyone could.

I began to really pay attention to all of my thoughts. When I was alone. When I was with people.

I noticed that I really thought very differently "behind closed doors" if you will, than what I actually portrayed to the world. It's safe there, right? We feel safe to say exactly what we really think when we think no one can hear us think it. But-- would you think it if they could hear you?

The same is true with our imagination. Guys, ever undressed a woman with your minds eye while standing right in front of her? Ever go further than that with your thoughts and imagination? Would you be so forward if she could hear your thoughts, and see what you are seeing inside where you think it's safe?

God sees it all!

Let me say that again, God sees it all!

God actually does see our imaginations and knows every thought.

As I began to watch my own thoughts, I realized what a hypocrite I really was. My favorite quote is: "Our character is determined by what we do when no one is looking."

What do we do when no one is looking? Are we the same person when we think no one is watching as we are in the public eye? I was not! This had to change!

This now became my new everyday task, to watch both my thoughts and my actions when I thought I was "behind closed doors." I learned a lot about myself. How judgmental I was. How proud I was as I thought of myself so much more highly than those around me. We all do it if we are honest with ourselves. I learned how two-faced I was. Just like my friend said, "They say nice words to my face, but I can hear the truth in their thoughts and it hurts."

I was ashamed of what I discovered about myself. I cried a lot. Asked forgiveness a lot. Repented a lot. I asked God to help me. How could I transform my thoughts to honor him? I desired a clean conscience before Him and wanted to be pure in my heart towards both God and man. Purifying my thoughts, taking every thought captive to love, was THE greatest advancement in my personal transformation.

He began a great work in me and gave me some wonderful tools. I'll share them with you now.

First tool.

He took me to 1 Corinthians 13: 4-7

Love is Patient, Love is Kind. It does not envy, it does not boast, it is not proud. It does not dishonor

others, it is not self-seeking, it is not easily angered,
it keeps no record of wrongs. Love does not delight
in evil but rejoices with the truth. It always protects,
always trusts, always hopes, always perseveres.

He had me break it down and focus on just one section at a time.

Love Is Patient

He wasn't content with me learning to be patient with others, but with myself as well. I was to evaluate my thoughts to see if I was being patient with others *and* myself.

Adding to that, He told me one time, "I will judge your love for me, by your love for your husband and those in your household, before I will judge you for your love for strangers." Ever notice how much nicer you are to a stranger who bumps into you or gets in your way than how you treat your spouse or children? I noticed that my tone of voice and patience was not up to a good standard when it came to my own family and that I would need a lot of work there. He wanted me to grow in becoming a servant, treating my husband and children as if they were Jesus Himself.
If I wouldn't speak to Jesus with certain tones of voice, then I shouldn't them. If they needed me to do something for them, I was to do it willingly with love, not grumbling or begrudgingly. Why do we get angry in the first place? Anger is almost always rooted in selfishness.

Anger became a marker for me. If I was getting angry, I was NOT in patience. I had to become an observer, like a third person watching the scene. Instead of being reactionary, reacting out of carnal instinct to everything happening around me, I would instead become an observer. As an observer, I could evaluate the situation tuned into God's Spirit. He would help me to see how I was behaving in light of His word. Did I respond to people as one who is of heaven. If you wouldn't find the behavior in heaven, then it should not be in you on earth. We are to give all those around us a glimpse of the kingdom through our lives. We are a living epistle.

Anger and impatience shows the selfish heart. We want things our way. I would learn that in the majority of the cases, especially in the beginning, that it was me that needed to learn to let go and let the other person have what they wanted, or let them win an argument. It is amazing to me just how much the self nature will fight to be the winner, or fight to have it's way and desire that everyone else serve them in various ways to make their life better. We tend to want what we want over the needs or desires of someone else. We will rationalize it all and find every reason why that person is undeserving of things and we are deserving.

***

Love Is Kind

Are my thoughts kind? Would others, if they heard my thoughts say that my thoughts were kind? Kind towards God? Kind towards my family? Friends? Strangers? And kind towards myself?

Come on ladies and gents, take a good look. Are you kind to yourself? This matters to God and it will change you in incredible ways when you can love yourself enough to be kind in your thoughts towards yourself.

In each of these areas of love, I would camp out there and evaluate my thoughts to see if I were measuring up. Every thought needed to be taken captive to the obedience of Christ. To the obedience of love.

This continued with checking my thoughts for envy, boasting, being proud. Did my thoughts dishonor others? Were my thoughts self seeking? It was at this point that God began to work on the servant's heart in me. Servants are not self seeking. They seek to serve and be a blessing to the lives of others, forsaking themselves. We already touched on this in Boundary 9, so I won't elaborate again here.

***

Love Is Not Easily Angered

There's that marker again. Love keeps no record of wrongs. I repeat: Love keeps no record of wrongs. This is another one that I spent time in my prayer room with God asking him to show me if I was keeping records. With much love, He would bring up people I had held unforgiveness toward and would elaborate on why I felt pain about it. It amazed me that the reasons I held record and unforgiveness was because I had not yet fully grown to live a sacrificial life for others. Until you are able to live sacrificially, *willing to suffer loss,* you will be offended when someone takes something from you-- whether they take an object or hurt your reputation (Boundary 4) or hurt your emotions (Boundary 9) or cause you to suffer loss in multitudes of other ways. Unforgiveness shows you are still in self. Be willing to suffer the loss. Be willing to let them go. God will judge them righteously at the appointed time. Our job is to live free from holding a record of wrongs.

It was yet another point that brought me closer to God in knowing His great love for me when I grasped that He too was holding no record of my wrongs. That was *not* what I felt my whole life in church. I had to camp out there and drink that in. God was not keeping a record. I actually remember one time when I was bringing up a past sin again to Him for the umpteenth time. He spoke to my heart and said, "Forget about it, I already did." My mind was blown. I was finally able to let it all go after that. Love keeps no record of wrongs.

***

Rejoicing with the truth

God brought another scripture to me here. It is *Philippians 4:8 Finally, Brother and sisters, whatever is true, whatever is noble, whatever is right, whatever is pure, whatever is lovely, whatever is admirable---if anything is excellent or praiseworthy---think about such things. NIV*

Right then He gave me a new list. Just as before, I began again. Now it had changed from things I needed to fix in my thoughts, to things I could think about and put into practice on another level.

Here is how it worked. Take that list and look at someone you know. Instead of seeing their faults, now you will look at them and see, whatever is true, noble, right, pure, lovely, admirable, excellent or praiseworthy, think about those things. At first, you may have to dig if you are having a difficult relationship with them. But this is how you begin to see gold in everyone. We are told to edify, encourage and exhort people. This is how it is done. When you think on these things as you look them, you bring these qualities to the forefront in your heart. You will speak to them from this place and bring forth life and the gold that is there.

Take the list and look at God. You will see if your relationship with Him is skewed. You must always look at Him to see what is true, noble, right, pure, lovely, admirable, excellent and praiseworthy. Think on these things.

Finally, take this list and look at yourself. Find the gold. Love yourself. See what is true, noble, right, pure, lovely, admirable, excellent and praiseworthy. Think on these things. Love yourself in your thoughts. You will become what you behold.

The last tool He gave me was, the fruit of the Spirit.

Galatians 5:22-23 But the fruit of the Spirit is love, joy, peace, forbearance, kindness, goodness, faithfulness, gentleness and self-control. Against such things there is no law.

To continue this work on my heart, He led me to evaluate my heart, my feelings, thoughts, emotions, and outward works on this fruit.

Forbearance (patience). There it is again. Must be important.
Was I patient? Was I patient with God? Patient with myself? Patient with others?

Kindness: Was I kind in my thoughts and actions towards God? Kind to myself? And kind to others?

Goodness: Was I good? My conscience would tell me. Was I good towards God? Good towards myself? And good to others?

Faithfulness: Was I faithful to God? Was I faithful to myself? Was I faithful to others? If not, then work on becoming faithful. You have to put these into practice. Practice makes perfect.

Gentleness: Was I gentle? Tender? Gentle and lowly in how I came before God? Was I gentle in how I thought and acted towards myself and to others? If not, work on that.

Self-control: I am still working on this one--just being honest. Self control touches everything. Do I have control over my actions? Over temptations? Over my mouth and what comes out of it?

Out of the overflow of the heart does one speak. If you pay attention to your thoughts, they will reveal what is really in your heart. They are the window in, who you are at your core. The evidence of what is in your heart will come out through your words and your actions, which is your fruit. God looks at the heart of a man. He said, "You will know them by their fruit." Matthew 7:16

Fruit is what you see of a person's life over time, what is consistently true and evident about them. You can get a look at what other people see when you hear what they say about you. Do people tell others, Oh he is so patient! She is so kind! She has such great self-control. He is so faithful and gentle-hearted. What is your fruit?

If you will take the time to develop your heart in this way, you will literally experience life, God and people differently.

Love, joy and peace will be your consistent life experience as all the wrong thoughts that tormented your mind and heart, separating you from God, are gone.

Continuing with The Heart

I would discover something fantastic after doing this work of cleaning my heart and purifying my thoughts. The logs had been taken out of my own eye, I could now see clearly how to help with what was in someone else's eye (heart).

What was fascinating to me was, because I had taken the time to focus on my own logs and did the hard work needed to remove them, I was filled with compassion for those who had a speck or log in their eye.

Before all of this work to change my thoughts and my actions, I judged. I judged myself harshly and therefore, I judged you harshly.

All these boundaries touch. It was as I put them all into practice in relationship with God, that I learned He was not judging me, and didn't want me to judge myself so harshly. Because I felt God's extraordinary love in patience and kindness toward me as I grew in self discovery, my heart was softened by His goodness toward me. I felt safe. God doesn't desire to judge us or punish us. He desires to set us free! He desires to work with us toward our full sanctification. And I discovered He was extremely patient and kind as I looked to Him to sort it all out. This caused me to grow in patients, kindness and goodness towards myself in my imperfections and weaknesses, and this then followed through to others. I no longer saw others weaknesses or imperfections as things to judge harshly, but saw them as areas that needed a touch from Jesus. Whatever Jesus touches gets healed.

I also learned that not everything was my business to touch. No one had to tell me about my logs. God did. In His timing, as He grew me, He would show me. Sometimes, He wants us to help others see their logs/specks, but only by His leading and only from a heart that truly loves the individual and wants to bring about healing. God demonstrated this to me by bringing me very special friends who walked very closely to God and had His heart. They would at times help me to see what I could not see in myself. But it was always done with so much love and compassion that it never felt like they were finding fault. We were simply sharpening one another according to God's word.

Even as I write this I feel the soft gentleness of God's love for us. In closing this chapter, understand that this work was done over months and even years of time. I spent time on each area and put it into action in my life before moving on to the next one. It is too overwhelming to do it all at once. Work on one at a time until you feel you are ready to take on the next. In this way, you are living it out by experience and it will not be lost on you as only words, but as a living truth.

May I pray for you?

Father, it is my prayer that each one reading these pages discovers how incredible Your word is. That if we follow the precepts you have laid out, we can walk in extraordinary freedom, authority and power in Christ Jesus. I pray You help them just as You helped me, to sit down with each of these lists and one by one, evaluate our own heart in the presence of Your Holy Spirit to be led by Him. In Jesus' name, Amen

Boundary 13: End-Goal Oriented--Stole My Joy

Don't worry about anything; instead, pray about everything. Tell God what you need, and thank him for all he has done. Then you will experience God's peace, which exceeds anything we can understand. His peace will guard your hearts and minds as you live in Christ Jesus. Philippians 4: 6-7 NIV

Because this book is sharing what I had to overcome to be able to evangelize and grow in relationship with God, that is the area of stress that I am going to cover here.

It took having a friend around me all the time to recognize that I pretty much lived stressed out. I was end-goal oriented.

It didn't matter what I was doing, I had to get there. I had to get to the end goal. When I was training and showing dogs, I stressed about all the training that had to get done and be done perfectly so that I could be successful at competition. I ate, drank and slept training, showing and competing. I stressed about bloodlines, studying them day and night. I imported my dogs from all over the world to get the very best dogs in my program. I stressed about what food they ate, how much exercise they got, socializing them, and getting every title I could on both ends of their name. Both champions and proven workers. That meant impressing judges. I did all my own lab work, got all sorts of health clearances and certifications, did my own promotions of my dogs and kennel, including building and maintaining a web site, building and maintaining a functioning boarding and grooming kennel and so much more.

My mind was always on the end goal of getting the next title to prove their value or to produce the highest quality dogs who could do it all.

Training my horses was the same. I went out to ride on any given day to get to an end goal. I had an agenda.

This trend continued when God called me to start praying for the sick. The end goal was to see people get healed. It was to gain the next gift or ability in Christ so that I could do more. When I saw God moving in other people's lives with gifts and anointings, I cried.

> 1. Because I had never seen it in church people before. I was so amazed and overwhelmed to see all that God was still doing in His people today.
> 2. Because I wasn't walking in the gifts yet, I thought I must be too dirty for God to use in such ways. (Boundary 3: Sins Disqualified Me)
> 3. I thought I wasn't good enough, clean enough, pure enough, loved enough or gifted enough to achieve the end goal. I questioned, what was possible? What would God actually do through me?

At this time, I had met people who walked in extraordinary gifting: Seeing in the Spirit; Knowing what was wrong with people before they told them; Knowing intimate details of people's lives without knowing them; I saw people who flowed in great levels of the gift of healing and I met people who were led by the Spirit in ways that boggled my mind. The intimate relationships they had with God were interactive and palpable.

This created an insatiable hunger in me to make sure I was clean and worthy for God to do such things with me as well. I didn't understand yet the power of righteousness in Christ Jesus. I was still very much works oriented. If I worked hard to be good and clean, maybe God would let me do what my new friends could do. Being good and clean is important. It's very important. Cleansing my heart proved valuable in many ways. But it wasn't what was needed to move in power with God; faith was. And what I believed in my heart was. Not faith in myself or my gifts or abilities, but faith in Jesus. Faith in who He is and what is available in Him and through Him.

God is moved by faith. Our greatest limitation is our own minds. We will only walk in as much as we believe we can.

Moving on. The end-goal mentality was robbing me of something.

Joel Sweeney, said something that was profound for me one day. He said, "Lisa, The joy is in the journey." He even bought me a wall hanging that said it so I wouldn't forget.

What Joel was trying to show me, was that I was so focused on fixing my heart to be accepted by God (not recognizing I was already accepted in Christ Jesus), putting in countless hours of self evaluation and purification, stressing about the end goal, that I was missing out on experiencing the moment I was in. I was so focused on growing into a gifting or getting someone healed that I was missing out on enjoying the journey to getting there.

We are told not to worry. Not to live in fear. And Joel's simple words, "The joy is in the journey" became my new life motto. I had to learn to slow myself down and actually experience the moment I was in, no longer thinking, "I'll be happy when…(fill in the blank of goals that had to be met)", But realizing that I could LIVE happy, enjoying every moment. I could allow myself to experience the moment I was in as a journey with God. It was something we were traversing along together and I could trust that each moment and day were enough for that moment and day. It was OK to simply be me--as I was--on a journey to wherever it was that God was taking me as I trusted in Him.

I could breathe.

We are to run our race as though to win. We think the end goal is to win that race. But what if winning the race is the journey itself? Enjoying the training that gets us there; enjoying learning how to become our best; enjoying the sights, sounds, and smells on the path each day; enjoying the people we will meet; even finding joy in the pain as we train ourselves to become stronger; or occasionally get injured as we run this race of life. Yes, when you are working towards an end, even the pain is pleasant because we know pain brings forth growth.

The journey is the race. Our joy is in the journey.

***

Father, thank you for freedom from fear and worry. You shared with us in Your word that we are to live for today. Thank you for Your joy! The joy of the Lord is our strength. Help us to slow down, to look around us and see the beauty of the journey we are on. Yes, at times the journey is difficult, even painful. But with you by our side, we can experience peace and joy, finding happiness in all things. Help us Lord to find that our joy can be found in the journey, In Jesus' name, Amen.

Boundary 14: Negativity

Finally, brothers and sisters, whatever is true, whatever is noble, whatever is right, whatever is pure, whatever is lovely, whatever is admirable-if anything is excellent or praiseworthy-think about such things.
Philippians 4:8

How do you rate yourself? Mostly positive? Or mostly negative?

As we have discussed in previous chapters, our thoughts are powerful. What you think has an incredible impact on how you live out your life. I had been a mixture of both negative and positive. They warred against each other in so many ways that it would cause me to flow in neutral (not going anywhere) until I got my thoughts sorted out and gravitated into positive.

There was a season in my life, years ago, when I found myself so deep in the land of negativity that my husband got really mad one day and said, "I don't know why I even talk to you! No matter what I say, you find the negative in everything," as he went outside slamming the door behind him.

I just stood there_____I knew he was right.

It's weird because I knew I had gotten extremely negative. I even hated it about myself, but didn't have the power or determination to change until someone vocally told me to my face that it was a big issue that was affecting them and our relationship.

That day was a turning point. After maybe 10 minutes, I humbled myself. I followed after my husband who was outside fixing the roof on our camper. I told him I was sorry for how I had been behaving. That I hated it within myself and that I was going to do my best to change.

Negativity has much power when embraced. It creates an atmosphere for failure, depression and low self worth. It makes statements such as-- I can't. I won't. I shouldn't. It's too hard. I'm not able. You're not able. Nothing good will come of it. It'll cost too much, fall short of expectations, cause damage, hurt me, be rejected. I'm not smart enough, pretty enough, good enough, talented enough. I don't have the resources. It'll take too long. People will dismiss me, abuse me, refuse me, confuse me, deny me, and the list can go on and on for infinity. We can find countless ways to be negative about ourselves, others, opportunities, and every activity under the sun. Negativity can take over if we embrace it as the lenses by which we choose to see everything.

How you live your life is a choice. The good news is: You can change yourself right now!

The next day after the encounter with my husband, I called my friend who also acted as my mentor during this season of growth and we talked about this. I want to give him credit here because this next bit of advice really helped me to develop strategies of change for future problems and boundaries that I would face. What I love about Joel, is that he always pointed me to God to seek Him for answers to my problems. He was always helping me to hear God for myself and develop an intimate, personal relationship with Him. He told me, "In each situation you come to, or for each person that you see in front of you, I want you to ask Holy Spirit to show you three positive things about it/them. Then, once you have those three things, I want you to act on them. Embrace and allow those three things to energize you to see the yes in what is in front of you. As for the people, I want you to tell them the three positive things you see in them. Bring out the gold you see. Become a gold digger."

This seems easy, but when you are used to finding everything negative about a person and this caused you a lot of dysfunction in your relationship, it can feel very awkward and uncomfortable at first to purposefully and genuinely tell that person the good you see in them with the intention of blessing them and edifying them. It was hard at first. Change isn't easy. We have to humble ourselves. We have to silence our ego and suck up our pride.

We can feel foolish as we purposefully choose to behave differently than what people are used to. But if we will simply be humble and maybe even tell them, "Hey, I'm working on changing the way I am. I want a new me." They will respect that and accept your honest attempts. Sometimes you will need to take a deep breath, and then just do it.

This homework from my friend worked amazingly. I've learned that this is the most important part of creating effective life transforming change within yourself. You have to be willing to do the homework of applying what you learn, be it from God's word, or from the teachers He sends you. You *have* to put in the work to get the change.

If you keep doing what you've always done, you'll keep getting what you've always gotten. The definition of insanity is to continue doing the same thing over and over expecting a different result to occur.

This advice also helped me grow in hearing God. I began to pause--to ask God what He saw in each situation, or in each person. I asked Him to show me three positive things. It worked! He did! This began the journey of transformation. I told God, "I want the spirit of Barnabas." Barnabas was known as an encourager. I wanted to be known as a great encourager.
He answered my prayer--But I had to participate in gaining the prize. Today--If you ask anyone who knows me, what are Lisa's strengths, I am positive that one of the top in the list will be that I am a great encourager.

As with all gardens, it takes time to plant new seeds and get through the seasons of growth before really good fruit can be seen.

It took time.

I had to be patient with myself as I battled the negative thoughts that would come trying to have a voice and endure the behavior of those around me as they continued to treat me according to my past fruit. It took around 7 months to a year before enough people had experienced the new me consistently enough that they accepted the change and responded in kind. This can be frustrating at first. So, keep this in mind as you progress in becoming a new you. You will have to suffer loss and expect to be treated less than you hope for until your new fruit is seen as unwavering and consistently true about you.

When you give permission for negativity to rule you, and you have done so for many years, it will not give up it's voice willingly. It will fight to remain. God's word says, "Submit yourselves, then, to God. Resist the devil and he will flee from you." James 4:7 NIV

First, submit yourself to God. Come under His care. Listen to His guidance and be lead by His Spirit. Second, resist the devil. The way you resist him in this case, is to give it no mind. Ignore the negative thoughts. Let them simply float on by and give them no place. Don't take hold of them. Don't embrace them or meditate on them.

God's word also says in 2 Corinthians 10:5, "casting down imaginations, and every high thing that exalteth itself against the knowledge of God, and bringing into captivity every thought to the obedience of Christ;" (KJV)

Take every thought captive to the obedience of Christ. Christ is love. Are your thoughts loving--not sensual love, but true, pure, Godly love? If you are having trouble with that and wonder what kind of thoughts you can embrace to have effective change, go to Philippians 4:8 "Finally brothers and sisters, whatever is true, whatever is noble, whatever is right, whatever is pure, whatever is lovely, whatever is admirable-- if anything is excellent or praiseworthy--think about such things." (NIV)

Again, you will need to literally set aside time to focus your thoughts. The "whatever" in the scripture means to focus on *anything* that is true (actually true), like God's word. Focus on anything that is noble. What comes to mind? Look at it. Ponder it. See nobility in your life, in your walk. Become noble. See everything that is right and good. See yourself as right and good as you are in Christ, free from all that bound you. Focus on things that are pure. Take the time to look for purity. Then become pure in your thoughts and actions as you conform to purity. Focus on all that is lovely, admirable, excellent and praiseworthy. Become lovely; become admirable in all you think, say and do. Become excellent. Become praiseworthy.

What you keep steadily before your eyes is what you will become. You will become what you behold. Embrace these things. Behold them. Never let them out of your site. Give negativity no voice or power to influence your life in any way.

Begin to use positive affirmations--I can and I will. I am able. I am good. I am kind. I am smart. I am faithful. I am strong. I am powerful. I am determined. I am a peacemaker. I am victorious. Nothing is impossible for me. I am able to do all that I see before me. I am loving. I am honorable. I am noble. I will change the world for the better. I am a go getter. I see good in all that I meet. I am an empowerer as I am empowered.

Can you feel the difference just reading that? Now for your homework. Get a piece a paper or two and fill it in front and back with your new "I am's."

God said His name is, I AM THAT I AM. Your I am is powerful! Who do you say you are? Whatever you consistently say you are, you will bring to pass. Write out who you want to be. When I did this, I was NOT YET the things I put on my list. I wasn't yet patient. But I put down, "I am patient. I was not yet as kind as I wanted to be. But I put down, "I am kind." We speak those things that are not yet as though they ARE. That is FAITH! You are prophesying it into being in your life. So write down all the things that you are not yet, but wish to be. Then, every single morning, go to a mirror and read the list out loud to yourself. Begin to see it. Believe it. And walk it out by faith!

You are able to do all things through Christ you strengthens you.

Father, I thank you that today negativity is crushed under his/her feet. That he/she feels empowered to put these things into practice by following the truth in Your word that we can take every thought captive to be obedient to Christ, that we can focus on good things and so be changed, that we can resist the voice of the devil and listen instead to the voice of Your Spirit. The sons of God are led by the Spirit of God. Let us be so led. Give us the strength to follow You without wavering and develop the habit of focused change. I ask that You consistently send encouragement to each one as they choose this new blessed reality for their lives. In Jesus' name. Amen

Boundary 15: What You Believe

"What do you mean, 'If I can'? Jesus asked.
"Anything is possible if a person believes."
The father instantly cried out, "I do believe, but help
me overcome my unbelief!"
Mark 9:23-24 (NLT)

What you believe and accept as truth, is powerful!

While this verse (Mark 9:23) is talking about the casting out of an evil spirit, I want to use it to show that what you believe or do not believe has great power to determine the course of your life. Notice there is a very powerful tiny two letter word in verse 23; "if". Jesus said, "What do you mean, **if** I can? Anything is possible **if** a person believes." (Emphasis added)

Early in the year, 2019, I made a grand declaration to myself and others that I was going to go from "couch potato" (having never run a race in my life) to completing a 50K Ultra Marathon (31.07 miles) in 9 months. It wasn't said in arrogance, but from a great desire to overcome some long standing personal boundaries. Boundaries had become my nemesis. The process of accomplishing this high goal was packed full of boundaries I needed to conquer to advance to a greater place of freedom and strength. Strength of body, mind, character and spirit.

I bought a journal to track my journey with; on the cover it says, "I can and I will--watch me." I also have a vinyl script that I put on my daughters bedroom door. Being at the end of our hallway, it's always there to be seen daily, it reads, "She believed she could, so she did." I had learned that what you keep before your eyes will develop what you believe. So, I wanted positive affirmations everywhere I looked.

As you have probably guessed, I did it!

It wasn't easy. As a matter of fact, it was one of the hardest things I have ever done in my life. The key ingredient to my success, however, was that I believed that I could and refused to accept a different truth as far as it was possible with me. I changed how I spoke. Instead of saying, "I think I can do it", I said, "I will do it."

My thoughts go to the Wright brothers who believed that man could fly. Though everything was stacked against them and everyone around them doubted them, they believed. The same with Thomas Edison: he believed that he could create a light bulb that could harness the power of electricity in such a way that it was gentled down, sustained in a globe that would provide safe light and get us away from open flames as that source of light. He failed over 10,000 times, and then--success. All because he believed.

Belief, when it is owned by the heart as truth, becomes unwavering faith. When you have this level of faith, you will act on it. You will continue to act on it until it becomes reality. The part you must remember here is, it goes both ways. You may hold tight and act upon a wrong belief just as strongly, and at times more strongly, than a correct belief. You will put action to what you have faith/belief in.

This book, "Breaking Through Boundaries", is meant to crush the power of wrong beliefs. It was only when I believed the power of God was not for today that I walked without that power. It was only when I believed my sins disqualified me that I became trapped in fear, shame and condemnation. When I changed that belief to the truth, that Jesus paid for it all and that my belief in Him was enough to set me free and make me righteous, I was now qualified to do all I saw before me. I had been free and qualified through Jesus all along. Wrong belief had me trapped in a jail cell that had no lock on the door. That wrong belief became cement shoes.

***

Each boundary is a belief. Each belief has the potential to be a boundary--or your key to freedom.

As you have noticed in the preceding 14 chapters, each boundary was a belief system. The keys to overcoming these traps are:

1.Recognize that you have a belief.

2. Evaluate the belief. Is it liberating you, expanding you, or limiting you? What do I believe? Why do I believe it?

3. Search for the truth. The truth shall set you free.

This is the tricky part. Most of the time, we think our current beliefs **are** the truth. We accept our current beliefs as who we are and that we can't change. It is my hope that after you have read this book, you will see how a belief can seem like the truth until you learn to pause, step back and observe what you believe, and seek God's Spirit to guide you into all truth. Is what you believe the truth? The greatest indicator that you have been deceived is that you will feel you are in bondage. There is a boundary in your belief that keeps you from being able to do anything you set your mind to.

Everything in your life experience is tied to what you believe in every given moment.

What do you believe?

Some examples to get us started:

I am not smart enough	vs	I am smart enough
I can't change	vs	I can change
I'll be rejected	vs	I'll be accepted
I'm limited	vs	I am limitless and resourceful
I'm not equipped for the task	vs	I can become equipped
I am too short to reach that high	vs	I can get a ladder!
I destroy relationships	vs	I will build relationships
I don't deserve love	vs	I deserve love and give love

I am not worthy	vs	I am worthy
I can't do anything right	vs	I can do anything I set my mind to with excellence
It's too hard	vs	It's a challenge I'm ready for
I don't matter	vs	I am valuable and an asset
I am only one person, I can't make a difference	vs	My voice has power and I intend to change the world for the better

Beliefs have the power to change your attitude--the power to cause you to walk in power and strength, or as a weak whipped puppy.

Beliefs can be prophetic. If you **believe in your heart** that people will reject you, you will give off that body posture, you will say things that will cause rejection, you will self destruct and in return, you will be rejected. But, if you change your belief to that of being accepted wherever you go, you will walk as one who is accepted, you will accept others, you will give off an energy that causes others to say, "I want to be around him, her," and this too will come to pass. Well--as long as what you want accepted is acceptable. If you have been trying to be accepted while offering bad behavior, you will find it a long struggle. But when you change to become what is acceptable (we are only commanded to love), then you will receive the harvest from what you have planted.

Belief is everywhere. You believe that when you sit on a chair that it will hold you up. You believe it so much, you don't even think about it, you just sit. You believe that when you flip on a light switch that the light will come on. You have faith/belief that when you drive down the road at 60 miles per hour, although the car in the next lane is coming at you from the opposite direction also going 60 mph with only a few feet between you as you pass one another, that it's safe to do that, over and over again. If you didn't believe those things, you might not do them.

When I went skydiving for the first time this year, I believed the instructor knew what he was doing. I believed the plane would fly just fine and the pilot was capable. I believed that my parachute would open. I believed it was going to be one of the best experiences of my life. I believed I would land just fine and if I didn't, I believed I would instantly meet my best friend, Jesus. Either way it was going to be an awesome day! It was! It was one of the most amazing experiences of my life.

For others, it was terrifying. Why? Because they believed it would be.

***

You can change what you believe about yourself.

I want to give you a bit of homework that I use for myself to change what I believe about myself, and as a result, change my personality. This is super cool and special, you have the power to change what you believe. You have the power to redesign yourself. First, you need to give yourself permission to be happy. Give yourself permission to be successful. Give yourself permission to be loved. Give yourself permission to be amazing!

Some of the greatest and most famous people (my mind goes to Zig Ziglar as one of many), used positive affirmations to transform themselves into what they wanted to be. I too adopted this and continue to write new ones to advance myself on my progressive journey. Positive affirmations are a way to reprogram yourself to believe for something new. Many of these things are not yet true about you. That is what faith is for. It is to believe for things that are not yet as though they are right now.

Positive affirmations may be:
I am the kindest person I have ever met.
I am self driven to be a success at everything I do.
I am prompt and punctual.
I am a great communicator.
I am likable.
I am generous.
I wake up every morning with a smile on my face.
I am confident.
I am a go-getter.
I am willing to do things others won't.
I believe that impossible is only a word. It's definition does not pertain to me.
I seek ways to create positive change.
I am able to do all I set my mind to.
I am worthy to be loved.
I am worthy of success.
I am worthy of being happy.
I am blessed and I am a blessing
I am favored and I show favor.

That was a very short list. Usually when I get going on a new affirmations list, it will be around 4 sheets of paper long. What you are doing is writing out those things you wish you were, or that you currently are, but want more of it to be at the forefront of your identity.

If you are like me, in the beginning, it felt like I was lying. It felt uncomfortable to say things I knew were not true about me yet.

Keep in mind, we are transforming ourselves to become what we are <u>not yet</u>. This is what faith looks like. You speak those things that are <u>not yet</u> as though they <u>are now</u>.

It looks like this, take the time to write out your affirmations pages. Write out every quality that you want to be. How do you want to present yourself? How do you want people to see you? What do you want your new personality to be? What kind of people do you want to draw to yourself? How successful do you see yourself?
Every quality you hate about yourself, affirm the quality you want now. Describe the new you. Precious, positive, punctual, persevering, powerful. Now there's an idea, if you get stuck a bit, go down the alphabet and use it to find adjectives to describe who you want to become.

Once you have your list, put it in the bathroom or bedroom. Somewhere there is a mirror. Now, every single day, you are going to get up and look yourself in the eye and tell yourself **who you are!!**

I know I shared to do affirmations in another chapter, but these chapters are meant to stand alone and this is a powerful way to create change. You will be amazed at how in time, you will actually become this person. You are a creative being. God said His name is, "I AM THAT I AM." You have **power** in your I AM, made in God's image, who you say you are is who you will become if you believe it by faith and put action to your words.

If you say, "I am kind." believe it and start implementing ways to be kind.

If you say, "I am punctual." believe it and start making sure you are punctual. If you struggle, ask God to help remind you to stay on target.

God is with you. Seek Him to lead you and guide you to becoming who you really are! It all starts with what you believe.

***

Let the chapters in this book prime the pump that will begin to show you your own personal boundaries. As you journey on, let's pray.

Father, thank you for creating us in your image. We are the only living beings on planet earth that you gave free will to choose what we will believe. You created us to be creative. This means being creative in changing ourselves as well-- who we want to be, what we want to become, and what we accept as truth. Help us to see what has put concrete on our feet. Help us to see clearly what beliefs we hold that are not true, and give us the truth that will set us free. Lead us, guide us, comfort us along the way. Empower us to be brave and change, not worrying what man thinks. Not worrying about our reputation during the process, but to walk strong and just go for it and change to be all we were born to be. Open our hearts to see what you see and let every lie and deception be broken off forever. In Jesus' name, Amen

The Boundaries Hid a Simple Truth

Over the course of 10 years, God has been developing me to overcome the boundaries that were set up in my heart. The culmination of it has brought me into a place of freedom and peace. Sadly, most people don't know to even look for this level of freedom because they are blinded by the boundaries, the walls that keep them from seeing and knowing about the green pastures just on the other side.

You see, I didn't find peace in the things I initially thought were the end goal (What I initially thought was the greener pasture).
It wasn't found in gaining a title, gaining a ministry, gaining a good reputation, gaining gifts, anointing or abilities. It wasn't even found in the act of becoming pure, or fasting or praying. These things don't matter to God, not like you might suppose. They are simply tools in a tool box, intended to serve a purpose. God is not impressed with people who have titles or grandeur. He is not impressed that you are anointed (with the anointing He gave you) or walking in the various gifts (that He gave you). He isn't impressed with how many hours you put into it all or how many people come to your gatherings. He's not impressed simply because you've learned to walk the walk and talk the talk.

I used to think I HAD to go out on the streets and use the gifts to touch people or I might make God upset that I was wasting what He had taught me was the children's bread--to cast out devils and heal the sick. But one day, I was down about my performance. I felt like I was letting God down because I didn't always WANT to pray for the sick every time I saw one, and I felt like if I didn't get the conversation moved into a "move of God" that I was missing the mark somehow. It was all about performance. In my low moment, God spoke to my heart. He said, " Lisa, did you love them?"

His words hit me like a brick. My purpose in life was to love people. IF that became a moment where I got to pray for their healing--great! IF that became a moment to give them an encouraging word from God--great! But it might be more simple. It might be that they needed someone to see them that day and just say hi and smile warmly. That might be enough to change their whole day, and possibly their whole life.

I remember a day that happened just recently. I was at the supermarket and was getting ready to go to a self checkout, but a lady came out from her register and said, "I'm open." I normally like to self checkout (introverted), but I saw this as a moment from God, that He might be setting something up. So, I smiled and said, "Great! Thanks!" and went into her line. As she was checking out my groceries, I said to her, "If you could ask God for anything you wanted today and knew He would give it to you, what would you ask for?" She thought for a second and then said, "Peace of mind."

Not gonna lie, I was disappointed. Just peace of mind? I was hoping she would want healing or something where God could move more spectacularly for her. I wanted to see a move of God.
I smiled warmly and said, "Give me your hand for a second." She gave me her hand. I said warmly, "Lord, bless your daughter today with peace of mind. Protect her Lord and give her the desires of her heart." I no more than got those words out of my mouth and she burst into deep sobbing right there in the store. I'm talking gut wrenching sobbing. Two co-workers ran up and looked at me with anger and said, "What did you do to her!?!" I explained that I simply prayed for her and it blessed her heart. They were not impressed. But I was! I got to see a much greater move of God than I had anticipated! She needed to know she was seen. She needed a moment of love!

It was selfish of me to want to see a grand move of God. But... I got just that! However, I had to eat a big piece of humble pie as God chastised my heart for pre-determining what a grand move should look like. I am addicted to seeing God move in love for people. He is real! He is alive! And I love for people to encounter Him in tangible ways. What I was learning, was God is just as moved by seeing us move in <u>love</u> as we are seeing Him move in some grand show of power. Love IS power!! God IS Love!

We are not commanded to walk in gifts or anointing. We are not commanded to have a title or ministry. We are commanded to love. The power, gifts and anointing will automatically flow from that place. But here is a caveat; life will be <u>so much more meaningful</u> when your love for others is genuine love, not manufactured. Manufactured 'duty' love is not good enough. Yes, it may get you some results. But most people can tell the difference. And *you* definitely will feel the difference. True love is not love out of duty or service. It is selfless. You genuinely love the person in front of you enough to sacrifice all that is needed of you (pride, reputation, etc) to make that person feel deeply seen, valued and loved.

Are you wondering how to go about loving others in your particular gifting? There are countless ways. Each of us has gifts from God given at birth. If you sing...sing for people because you love to bless them with that gift. Not so that *you* can be loved for your gifting. If you are an administrator, do it to make the lives of others easier, not just to be respected because of your gift. Do you have the gift of helps? Do it with a genuine heart to love people by making their lives easier. Do it as unto the Lord for His pleasure, not to be admired for your abilities.

Initially, I did everything for the wrong reasons. I had wrong motives and wrong beliefs. Life is a journey of never-ending learning and growth. But, I can tell you, the greatest freedom came when I learned how to love God without inhibitions, love myself without harshness or self-condemnation, and love my neighbor simply to love them with what I have without condition. That's the agenda--and it's no agenda at all. You are no longer *trying* to minister. No, it's a matter of the heart. You do it out of who you are. It's the overflow of your nature--your new born again God nature. I no longer looked for opportunities to use God's gifts for the sake of using His gifts to reveal Him. I looked instead for opportunities to love people in any way that I could. The use of the gifts comes second nature because it is who I am. I can't help but pray for their healing. I can't help but give them encouragement. It's who I am and what I love to do.

The weight is completely lifted off when you stop living life burdened with HAVING to do something. Now, you can enjoy the journey as you see the endless opportunities to reveal the God of love simply by being you and loving others with who you are and what you have in the moment.

***

1If I could speak all the languages of earth and of angels, but didn't love others, I would only be a noisy gong or a clanging cymbal. 2If I had the gift of prophecy, and if I understood all of God's secret plans and possessed all knowledge, and if I had such faith that I could move mountains but didn't love others, I would be nothing. 3If I gave everything I have to the poor and even sacrificed my body, I could boast about it, but if I didn't love others, I would have gained nothing.

4Love is patient and kind. Love is not jealous or boastful or proud 5or rude. It does not demand its own way. It is not irritable, and it keeps no record of being wronged. 6It does not rejoice about injustice but rejoices whenever the truth wins out. 7Love never gives up, never loses faith, is always hopeful, and endures through every circumstance.

8Prophecy and speaking in unknown languages and special knowledge will become useless. But love will last forever! 9Now our knowledge is partial and incomplete, and even the gift of prophecy reveals only part of the whole picture! 10But when the time of perfection comes, these partial things will become useless.

11When I was a child, I spoke and thought and reasoned as a child. But when I grew up, I put away childish things. 12Now we see things imperfectly, like puzzling reflections in a mirror, but then we will see everything with perfect clarity. All that I know

now is partial and incomplete, but then I will know everything completely, just as God now knows me completely. 13Three things will last forever—faith, hope, and love—and the greatest of these is love. 1 Corinthians: 1-13 NLT

***

In Conclusion

Overcoming these various boundaries will help you to grow into someone who is able to love others in a way that is healthy.

The hardest part will be to be willing to look at your own heart to accept and acknowledge that you have areas that need to change. The second part will be putting in the work needed to create a true transformation by changing your ways, changing your thoughts, changing what you accepted as truth; then, change how you live it out before God and man. Change is not easy and for many it causes great fear of the unknown.

Learn to live accepted (no fear of rejection).
Learn to live without a reputation (nothing to squash or elevate).
Learn to love all people without condition.
Learn to live with your hands wide open (God can both give and take away as He sees fit).

Learn to give the outcome of your days and your life fully into God's hands (let go of being in control, or demanding your way, let Him lead)!!
Live a life believing that you can accomplish all you put your heart into (nothing is impossible).
Learn to live a life trusting God (no matter what you see or don't fully understand).
And walking out your life feeling safe in The Father's care; It will set you free--free to love God, yourself, and others with your whole heart!

My closing prayer:

Father, thank you for all You have taught me. This book only covers maybe half of the boundaries I still need to write about. The kingdom is within us. Thank you for sending the Holy Spirit to help us get free from every boundary that keeps us from both experiencing the kingdom ourselves and from expressing it as it truly is for others to see. We are the living epistles of your word. We are the ambassadors of the kingdom. We are sent to reveal Christ and the kingdom. Thank you for grace to hear, to see, and to apply all You teach us by Your Spirit and to share it with the world. We are sons of God, led by the Spirit of God. In Jesus' name, Amen

The Sons of God

While all who are children of God are sons of God, there are some who stand out from the rest. We all have the opportunity to be esteemed in this group. It's a matter of the heart.

These sons of God are an elite group. They are willing to suffer great pain and personal loss for others and the kingdom, fearless in their resolve to complete the task God lays before them. They are the unshakable ones who have been and are being purified by fire--God's holy ones, set apart even from the "elite" of this world.

They are missionaries, warriors, fierce lovers of the heart of God and all He holds dear. They hate all forms of the work of the devil and crush it at every occurrence with wisdom and stealth. They are not of this world. They see as those who stand above it all, looking down on the earth from heaven's vantage point. They rule along with Christ as priest of the earth. The earth groans for them to be revealed. They are the keepers, the guardians, watchers that keep the world in check, masters of the heart, keen to seeing deceptions. They're willing to suffer great pain and loss for others. Their only reward is God's love and acceptance of them in the midst of their suffering. Only 1% of the church will walk as true sons of God. Suffering is their normal experience. They tend to be lonely, very misunderstood, abused verbally by both the lost and the church. They belong to no one. They are the sold out lovers of God, only moved by His Spirit and for His purposes. They are not swayed by man or earthly gains or rewards. They do not boast of themselves, but only of Jesus Christ and him crucified. Their reward is love. Yes, God himself, He is their portion, their bread and drink. Only He feeds their spirits and sustains them. The spirit world fears them. Angels are in awe of them. People on earth fear them and wish to destroy them. Even masses in the church want them dead because every darkness of the heart is exposed by them. They are the light bearers, fully engulfed by the light of Christ in them. They hate all sin or darkness in themselves and are willing to suffer the purging fires of God over and over and over again to be free from it. Catalyst. They start fires wherever they go. All wood and stubble get burned away as they walk by. They are anointed ones, carriers of the cross, dead to themselves, alive for Christ alone. Nothing on earth has the power to tempt them. They are in love with only one--Jesus Christ and none other! They wage war daily on all that is not godly, and leave peace in their wake. God holds back nothing from them for they live as slaves to his purposes. They give themselves into bondage of his love and walk as freemen--free from all forms of bondage known to man. Incorruptible. Unwavering in who they are and what they are alive for. Unshakable because they have already submitted themselves to the shaking of God's judgment. Clothed by God Himself in armor. God loves his sons. He broods over them. He watches them and protects them. No one can harm them without His permission and for His purposes. God is their jealous lover. He is their fierce protector and shield. They listen always for His voice and He speaks to them. They have free access to His throne and He imparts hidden knowledge to them there. Each has their orders to impact the earth and the people there on, in their own unique gifts and callings. They are never envious, jealous or covetous of another's gifts or calling because they understand their own. They know their value and purpose and equally value the value and purpose of others. No one feels either above or below his brother. They work as one--a well oiled machine. They take care of one another without batting an eye or considering the cost. Faithful to God and the family. Life is not something they hold tight. It is willingly given for others without hesitation. Everyone is seen as of great value and worth the cost that they suffer. Righteousness is written across their breast plates. Truth is imprinted wherever their feet land. They are humble and full of grace. The earth celebrates their coming as life emits from them wherever they go. Healing happens in all its forms. They are content to be nameless and of no reputation. They live only for Christ, to bring Him glory. They will appear as unimpressive. You may not even realize you were talking to one until they are gone and you are left feeling full of hope, joy and peace. The light of Christ in them remains on you and around you. Wake up sons of God! Rise up! A new day is dawning! It is time beloved for the sons of God to be revealed!

Matthew 5:9 blessed are the peacemakers for they will be called sons of God.

Romans 8:14 for all of those who are allowing themselves to be led by the Spirit of God are sons of God.

Lisa Beth Adams
#ChangeTheWorld
#GoBeLove

ABOUT THE AUTHOR

Lisa Beth Adams is a wife of twenty-seven years and a mother of 3 beautiful daughters. What makes Lisa stand out, is her insatiable hunger to know God and to enjoy the fullness of what a relationship with Him can be while here on earth. This drive has caused her to try things most Christians wont. She has consistently chosen to step past fears and perceived limitations to find the more of God. In this process she has learned how to listen and be led by the Spirit of God in the vast ways that He speaks, and by trusting this leading she has learned how to cooperate with Him, putting the precepts of God's Word into applied use to overcome limitations and former religious teachings that had her bound.

Lisa walks in fearless faith. She believes wholeheartedly that God is love and He wishes to reveal Himself to mankind through His body of believers in power and authority in depth of relationship with Him.

Lisa's relationship with God is something to be desired. She lives a laid down life. Having no desire for a reputation of her own allows her to speak straight from her heart without holding back, offering a way for others to learn and grow from her mistakes as well as from her obedience.

Deemed a catalyst by her peers. One of her stand out qualities is her ability to accelerate others into a greater fullness of their God given identity and to find a tangible, interactive relationship with the Living God. Her desire in this season is to write all she has learned so others can grow even higher than she. Letting her ceiling become their floor as they grow from glory to glory.

May God receive all the glory as we rise up becoming one with Him in all of our ways.

Made in the USA
Monee, IL
14 May 2020

30782035R00089